WISDOM is the principa
with all thy getting g

MW01615172

## DR. PRYOR'S
# LUCKY NUMBER
# MASTER
# DREAM BOOK

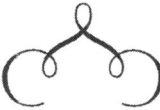

© CALLI CASA EDITORIAL, 2022

SUPERVISED BY VICTORIA REY
ILLUSTRATIONS: BERNABÉ PÉREZ

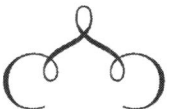

## PREFACE

Dear reader:

This book you have in your hands is different from other dream books because this book does not contain interpretations of dreams and hunches.

However, it does have a very detailed assessment of numbers associated to them, to help you find the numbers you need in your life to buy lotto tickers, to make decisions or find the perfect day to set important meetings or dates.

See what this Master Dream Book contains: Dr. Pryor`s Interpretations of Dreams and Hunches. American and Spanish First and Last Names in 1 to 100, 1 to 78 and 000 to 999 Combinations; Including Psalms for Various Conditions and Birthmonth Astrological Readings.

Enjoy!

Find Your Number

Words are interpreted in letters and in numbers both forms being symbols of ideas. The first nine digits are the roots of all numbers, and posses certain occult relationships.

## Key to Number Combinations

As every name may be the equivalent of a certain number so each letter, which composes the Name, has its own numerical value. These values are not without exceptions, but they have been used by the Rosicrucians and Kabalists from the earliest times, and are apparently derived from the Hebrew Alphabet. The following table shows the corresponding values of the English Alphabet, when compared to the numbers 1 to 9.

A = 1,  B = 2,  C= 2,  D = 4,  E = 5,  F = 8
G = 3,  H = 8,  I = 1,  J = 1,  K = 2,  L = 3
M = 4,  N = 5,  O = 7,  P = 3,  Q = 1,  R = 2
S = 3,  T = 4,  U = 6,  V = 6,  W = 6,  X = 6
Y = 1,  Z = 7

## Example How to find the Number

To obtain the numbers or digit for John George Brown, the following method is used. JOHN: J=1, O=7, H=8, N=5, the total is 21. Reducing this number to a single digit is done by adding 2 and 1 giving 3. GEORGE: G-3, E=5, O=7, R=2, G=3, E=5, the total being 25, the digit of 2 and 5 is 7. BROWN: B=2, R=2, O=7, W=6, N=5: the total is 22, 2 and 2 is 4.

The final result is as follows: John 3; George 7 and Brown 4. His number combination would be 3, 7, and 4. If one single number is required for the full name, add 3, 7 and 4 giving 14. 4 plus 1 is 5. John George Brown's single digit is therefore, 5.

# Guiding Psalms
## for Various Conditions

| CONDITION | PALM # | CONDITION: | PSALM # |
|---|---|---|---|
| Accusers | 54 | Failure | 12 |
| Advice | 27 | Family | 22 |
| Afflicted | 82 | Famine | 33 |
| Anger | 37 | Farming | 65 |
| Bad Luck | 23 | Fear | 31 |
| Bereaved | 23 | Finance | 9 |
| Bitterness | 27 | Flood | 69 |
| Blessings | 67 | Food | 28 |
| Blues | 31 | Forgiveness | 51 |
| Business | 38 | Friends | 38 |
| Children | 36 | Grief | 6 |
| Confession | 32 | Guidance | 27 |
| Confidence | 23 | Happiness | 16 |
| Contentment | 34 | Hate | 36 |
| Courage | 27 | Heartbroken | 34 |
| Court Case | 37 | Hunger | 146 |
| Crippled | 82 | Illness | 6 |
| Crops | 67 | Jail | 102 |
| Danger | 91 | Law Suit | 37 |
| Death | 23 | Lies | 31 |
| Delay | 38 | Lonely | 31 |
| Desires | 145 | Long Life | 91 |
| Disease | 6 | Love | 38 |
| Dreams | 73 | Luck | 67 |
| Enemies | 55 | Marriage | 19 |
| Evil | 34 | Mercy | 4 |

| CONDITION: | PSALM# | CONDITION: | PSALM# |
|---|---|---|---|
| Money | 9 | Sickness | 6 |
| Old Age | 71 | Sin | 41 |
| Pain | 116 | Slander | 31 |
| Peace | 27 | Sleep | 4 |
| Pity | 103 | Sorrow | 32 |
| Poor | 9 | Spirit Help | 51 |
| Power | 21 | Storm | 107 |
| Pregnant | 113 | Strength | 27 |
| Prison | 142 | Success | 27 |
| Prosperity | 27 | Thanksgiving | 30 |
| Protection | 5 | Travel | 46 |
| Rain | 147 | Trouble | 27 |
| Rest | 23 | War | 46 |
| Riches | 112 | Wealth | 112 |
| Sadness | 6 | Weary | 6 |
| Safety | 4 | What to do | 31 |
| Sailor | 107 | Wisdom | 103 |
| Salvation | 27 | Work | 90 |
| Servicemen | 65 | Worry | 23 |

May the Good and Merciful
Heavenly Father Hear and Grant this Prayer
for Peace, Success, and Happiness, Amen.

Dr. M. Pryor

"No man is blest by accident or guess,
True wisdom is the price of happiness."

Young

# A

12-22 A, 1-5-40—405
44-28 Abandon, 14-25-39—847
19-10 Abdomen, 3-13-22—126
06-14 Abolish, 32-46-51—786
27-92 Abortion, 37-55-68—984
46-55 Abroad, 7-9-11—663
21-88 Absent, 67-78-21—434
69-90 Abuse, 11-36-57—247
01-98 Academy, 60-69-76—506
18-07 Accent, 28-44-53—972
22-44 Accident, 3-11-72—532
04-08 Accordion, 4-8-18—488
16-96 Accuse, 21-37-55—498
69-79 Ache, 12-14-16—526
14-58 Acorn, 46-52-77—463
64-50 Acquit, 1-14-19—119
58-64 Acrobat, 68-73-12—106
63-14 Actor, 72-74-78—291
33-66 Actress, 1-2-4—860
73-59 Addict, 18-45-76-422
99-19 Address, 1-76-23—237
10-67 Admire, 45-49-57—779
86-98 Admit, 23-33-55—588
27-08 Adopt, 63-46-68—592
05-88 Adultery, 15-51-50—381
14-73 Advance, 31-43-59—467
34-36 Advice, 42-27-35—106
47-67 Affair, 19-37-51—444
26-98 Afraid, 27-36-78—261
91-92 African, 30-40-50—613
16-51 Afternoon, 7-12-24—324
39-40 Age, 15-41-18—666
04-10 Agent, 55-72-68—441

38-22 Agony, 72-37-43—144
96-21 Agree, 11-27-63—218
01-83 Agreement, 22-18-77—828
78-88 Air, 43-39-58—019
4-100 Airplane, 4-8-41—304
14-99 Alarm, 7-13-37—211
86-17 Albino, 10-17-45--414
19-39 Alcohol, 21-76-16—555
80-98 Aiderman, 4-9-11—987
12-44 Ale, 38-18-55—476
38-29 Alibi, 27-43-68—110
100-2 Alimony, 12-16-23—999
18-43 Alley, 67-71-78—412
43-93 Almanac, 4-14-46—415
06-30 Alone, 51-10-33—223
19-46 Alphabet, 31-19-67—685
22-36 Altar, 9-38-36—791
11-71 Ambulance, 57-71-73—883
86-99 American, 1-10-30—626
42-66 Ammunition, 27-38-5—421
18-71 Amulet, 47-51-36—894
14-44 Amusement, 12-37-5—438
76-93 Anchor, 8-12-39—011
87-98 Ancestor, 7-16-43—488
01-99 Angel, 1-14-69—376
26-43 Anger, 11-26-15—001
14-19 Animal, 14-49-44—494
67-84 Ankle, 22-48-53—227
29-14 Anniversary, 66-72-1—431
02-73 Annoy, 34-55-16—222
47-22 Anoint, 12-37-44—536
06-19 Answer, 60-53-78—559
37-89 Ant, 2-7-41—439
56-92 Antenna, 48-53-16—409
43-07 Antique, 8-68-72—511
6-100 Anxious, 26-43-58—667
10-25 Apartment, 46-78-62—335
66-78 Ape, 4-6-31—919
42-49 Apostle, 78-77-1—117
87-33 Appendix, 33-55-45—222
17-78 Appetite, 55-63-77—586
13-27 Applause, 15-52-63—331
55-33 Apple, 11-27-59—760
98-72 Application, 15-43-5—662
31-67 Appoint, 1-3-5—351
04-44 April, 61-52-63—201
49-18 Apron, 43-14-52—611
51-61 Argue, 56-22-37—105

32-59 Arm, 35-42-16—393
31-25 Armistice Day, 5-1-7—262
88-94 Army, 18-16-50—323
01-19 Aroma, 33-51-55—428
99-01 Arrest, 14-21-59—111
17-44 Arrow, 11-43-68—431
94-98 Artificial, 22-55-12—946
62-78 Artist, 15-27-74—521
23-53 Ashes, 66-78-70—638
19-87 Ask, 12-14-61—331
77-91 Asparagus, 49-69-55—817
14-17 Ass, 18-56-19—476
83-93 Assassin, 15-43-51—530
22-29 Assault, 53-67-14—522
07-44 Athlete, 36-41-53—999
12-23 Astrology, 12-24-36—553
1-100 Atom bomb, 1-3-78—632
43-26 Attack, 59-64-71—781
18-49 Attic, 32-43-51—668
26-87 Attorney, 16-59-68—166
43-99 Auction, 15-20-71—127
08-55 Audience, 1-8-32—116
17-33 August, 6-54-32—108
19-63 Aunt, 7-18-40—691
82-55 Automobile, 5-6-17—492
44-45 Autumn, 26-44-59—954
81-96 Avalanche, 20-30-70—779
02-49 Awaken, 4-10-61—146
18-61 Axe, 14-18-37—461

# B

62-87 B, 2-8-29—894
14-26 Baby, animal, 4-2-18—411
53-42 Baby, black, 13-32-50—530
19-55 Baby, white, 1-12-21—128
33-91 Baby, yellow, 4-35-56—563
43-27 Bachelor, 13-33-76—421
01-18 Bacon, 33-44-55—543
49-76 Badge, 6-16-43—331
15-18 Bag, 11-52-73—573
41-36 Baggage, 55-23-37—876
35-47 Bail, 36-42-51—427
56-72 Bake, 63-68-70—994
10-43 Baker, 22-47-65—762
7-100 Bakery, 10-17-60—117
76-93 Balcony, 52-55-31—523
27-56 Bald, 1-13-35—001
17-44 Ball, 14-27-55—487

44-71 Balloon, 44-69-35—271
08-53 Ball room, 8-18-28-812
16-11 Banana, 4-11-44—444
33-71 Band, 10-17-20—101
43-80 Bandage, 42-39-31—124
21-92 Bandit, 72-74-63—528
37-39 Banjo, 8-18-48-302
09-99 Bank, 4-5-54—455
14-55 Bankrupt, 42-73-76—799
78-87 Banquet, 18-42-53—663
05-67 Baptist, 5-11-55—810
19-53 Bar, 11-35-40—043
61-80 Barbecue, 33-55-61—816
93-97 Barber, 7-10-20—027
14-36 Barefoot, 39-42-50—345
23-42 Bargain, 20-18-66—206
77-66 Barge, 6-11-15—145
14-21 Bark, 6-16-40—400
08-11 Barley, 74-76-22—414
15-30 Barn, 43-33-53—882
40-55 Barrel, 14-22-36—991
99-04 Base, 3-4-1—114
09-13 Baseball, 9-16-66—619
52-14 Basement, 15-22-43—771
63-73 Bashful, 25-43-68—522
15-36 Basket, 8-16-24—458
44-61 Basketball, 26-8-42—882
70-80 Bastard, 20-50-69—431
48-21 Bat, 2-30-22—222
7-100 Bath, 36-69-70—367
15-61 Batter, 13-21-40—553
55-70 Battery, 28-40-66—782
01-99 Battle, 6-14-77—991
15-31 Beach, 9-15-62—434
36-42 Beads, 31-42-45—507
66-73 Beans, 13-16-19—180
52-89 Bear, 2-11-78—512
13-55 Beard, 19-66-78—221
55-76 Beat, 18-43-56—28
16-45 Beauty, 37-46-72—566
23-30 Bed, 1-62-70—910
36-70 Bedbug, 1-3-20—883
08-39 Bedsores, 4-44-74—044
16-42 Bee, 19-39-56—427
59-69 Beef, 10-16-77—933
63-77 Beer, 7-19-57—769
47-52 Beets, 8-18-48—212
16-41 Beggar, 1-3-8—477

16-78 Bell, 52-66-77—933
66-68 Belly, 18-33-26—889
37-43 Bellyache, 14-27-36—116
44-69 Belt, 27-33-39—427
14-92 Bench, 72-78-53—007
59-81 Bend, 19-43-56—766
06-14 Berries, 33-56-72—967
42-58 Bet, 76-77-68—438
27-45 Bible, 17-65-75—333
10-34 Bicycle, 3-45-72—807
13-26 Bill, 4-5-54—455
2-100 Billiards, 8-15-3—551
09-28 Bird, 4-2-22—224
30-50 Birth, 1-2-3—344
05-18 Birthday, 15-72-76—845
15-61 Biscuit, 1-12-22—321
53-87 Bite, 18-46-62—050
28-43 Black, 4-9-44—449
21-61 Black Jack, 21-6-59—171
73-77 Blanket, 18-43-50—566
54-86 Blaze, 53-26-37—113
41-90 Bleach, 47-57-68—315
8-100 Blind, 18-46-53—337
48-72 Blister, 3-5-14—107
12-21 Blonde, 15-20-25—525
20-50 Blood, 11-19-40—867
61-79 Blossoms, 43-41-48—484
05-40 Blue, 21-57-48—312
67-84 Bluff, 17-43-36—474
26-30 Blunder, 55-63-72—877
16-24 Blush, 13-17-27—444
08-88 Board, 4-44-54—404
53-74 Boarder, 19-23-46—221
41-91 Boast, 27-73-67—804
56-63 Boat, 11-33-18—131
30-50 Body, 19-36-42—421
42-76 Boil, 63-65-72—667
19-48 Bolita, 42-55-78—657
01-10 Bolipool, 19-37-45—678
86-99 Bomb, 2-6-19—113
15-43 Bonds, 46-52-73—527
32-66 Bone, 14-21-18—107
19-33 Bonus, 36-44-55—426
42-58 Book, 4-8-40—048
15-76 Boot, 15-33-78—412
23-46 Borrow, 12-26-43—518
15-27 Boss, 37-76-78—412
88-44 Bottle, 1-2-10—100

07-47 Bounce, 45-53-62—889
55-30 Bouquet, 67-73-14—913
09-22 Box, 15-16-40—114
43-26 Boy, 32-54-64—389
89-92 Bracelet, 3-9-14—880
76-54 Brains, 14-78-70—333
14-28 Brandy, 29-66-43—287
19-96 Brave, 13-55-65—773
87-43 Bread, 27-40-31—271
21-41 Breakfast, 2-27-69—216
66-46 Breast, 36-38-40—111
77-97 Brewery, 53-59-64—884
33-14 Bribe, 19-30-72—555
52-87 Brick, 43-36-46—188
21-12 Bride, 22-26-35—504
15-33 Bridegroom, 4-46-54—77
27-67 Bridge, 8-12-64—211
49-87 Bright, 30-40-50—343
01-52 Bronchitis, 26-18-44—52
43-21 Brook, 58-72-76—765
86-90 Broom, 14-55-59—514
06-66 Brother, 39-59-66—669
34-43 Brother'n-law, 6-9-14—383
17-20 Brown, 52-58-78—003
27-49 Bubble, 30-40-52—117
13-26 Bucket, 9-10-20—912
10-19 Bug, 53-64-74—893
43-67 Buggy, 22-14-8—991
55-71 Bugle, 10-11-27—802
7-100 Buick, 10-43-67—798
26-84 Building, 53-61-71—768
78-96 Bulb, 25-60-75—375
10-12 Bull, 6-11-66—166
22-36 Bullet, 27-43-61—132
16-26 Bullfrog, 10-12-14—411
19-38 Bump, 56-58-76—103
35-66 Bundle, 29-38-57—666
43-59 Burglar, 13-26-39—552
76-87 Bum, 10-14-61—116
93-12 Bus, 25-37-52—778
86-98 Bush, 68-41-21—4-12
100-3 Business, 69-73-74—519
47-77 Bust. 6-8-22—040
33-86 Busy, 24-48-16—884
15-33 Butter, 17-39-63—133
12-72 Butterfly, 53-65-70—912
94-86 Button, 64-68-77—682
04-09 Buzzard, 14-12-9—515

# C

22-03 C, 3-9-46—364
53-58 Cab, 27-30-40—004
92-96 Cabaret, 57-59-76—919
30-43 Cabbage, 32-16-59—761
15-56 Cabin, 19-38-45—582
01-98 Cactus, 43-37-53—333
25-50 Cadillac, 21-31-45—765
57-78 Cage, 16-56-76—004
68-43 Cake, 26-67-77—512
13-26 Calendar, 7-14-21—871
87-94 Calf, 27-29-54—119
15-31 CaH, 44-55-63—248
36-74 Calm, 19-38-53—554
55-67 Camel, 13-22-53—878
76-14 Camera, 15-37-62—913
08-44 Camp, 16-40-50—400
14-36 Can, 10-20-49—402
55-75 Canadian, 27-37-41—389
76-98 Canal, 29-39-49—549
3-100 Canary, 3-18-36—313
18-44 Cancer, 1-6-8—114
66-86 Candidate, 15-52-76—474
12-16 Candle, 26-72-12—597
55-96 Candy, 48-43-23—616
73-79 Cane, 1-11-28—101
15-66 Cap, 18-48-58—916
07-42 Capitol, 27-48-56—777
19-32 Capture, 26-38-54—199
56-88 Car, 6-10-20—16
48-52 Card, 48-52-13—333
07-13 Card Row, 11-12-13—123
01-05 Ace-Spades, 4-10-62—416
43-26 2-Spades, 4-53-71—457
52-48 3-Spades, 7-9-13—791
37-94 4-Spades, 2-7-10—271
26-80 5-Spades, 3-52-64—556
39-41 6-Spades, 10-1-17—111
53-92 7-Spades, 4-51-54—455
60-70 8-Spades, 1-11-64—116
27-85 9-Spades, 2-12-46—214
03-90 10-Spades, 8-45-48—844
15-77 J-Spades, 5-11-63—516
13-26 Q-Spades, 7-10-36—713
94-12 K-Spades, 8-33-60—836
15-37 Ace-Hearts, 11-65-66—187
26-49 2-Hearts, 3-11-40—413

50-70 3-Hearts, 8-29-70—297
41-91 4-Hearts, 5-15-23—512
18-55 5-Hearts, 20-14-12—211
59-83 6-Hearts, 18-35-73—137
33-66 7-Hearts, 10-22-25—122
18-58 8-Hearts, 71-62-66—766
92-98 9-Hearts, 39-47-59—345
1-100 10-Hearts, 4-21-27—422
06-46 J-Hearts, 15-7-8—788
18-58 Q-Hearts, 8-18-11—811
92-29 K-Hearts, 14-5-3—259
40-65 Ace-Clubs, 5-11-18—511
11-15 2-Clubs, 12-16-19—111
15-26 3-Clubs, 8-11-72—817
42-96 4-Clubs, 10-25-5—125
53-82 5-Clubs, 7-14-28—712
73-24 6-Clubs, 10-35-39—133
44-45 7-Clubs, 12-19-68—116
01-14 8-Clubs, 7-14-53—715
26-38 9-Clubs, 2-9-10—291
42-55 10-Clubs, 8-14-27—812
15-56 J-Clubs, 4-17-28—412
6-100 Q-Clubs, 7-17-75—717
30-42 K-Clubs, 3-42-43—344
56-74 Ace-Diamonds, 10-40—144
06-26 2-Diamonds, 10-6-7—167
14-55 3-Diamonds, 10-11-5—115
87-63 4-Diamonds, 9-19-32—913
98-42 5-Diamonds, 7-20-29—722
16-66 6-Diamonds, 3-4-2—234
23-35 7-Diamonds,; 12-68-6—166
42-56 8-Diamonds, 5-9-55—595
04-10 9-Diamonds, 71-21-6—726
15-36 10-Diamonds, 1-20-3—121
77-14 J-Diamonds, 14-4-5—145
33-52 Q-Diamonds, 77-1-7—717
13-23 K-Diamonds, 11-9-5—145
70-41 Cardgame, 1-15-37—568
32-61 Carriage, 9-19-69—051
83-30 Carpenter, 33-43-54—611
12-18 Carry, 12-15-36—822
73-91 Carve, 43-57-26—904
18-70 Cash, 27-78-72-444
42-55 Casino, 44-38-52—606
16-83 Casket, 54-26-38—576
42-61 Castle, 10-5-22—113
49-30 Caster oil, 7-5-64—553
14-24 Cat, 1-3-20—774

31-18 Catch, 18-43-27—650
97-43 Catholic, 56-23-39—769
9-100 Cattle, 6-11-66—826
43-51 Cave, 53-76-64—141
37-42 Ceiling, 76-43-21—563
06-14 Celebrate, 51-18-76—226
15-36 Cell, 43-31-52—524
98-99 Cellar, 38-45-66—643
62-84 Cemetery, 13-26-39—129
15-37 Cent, 1-5-10—107
08-15 Ceremony, 18-27-66—112
86-96 Chain, 23-47-72—458
22-47 Chair, 33-41-58—916
25-35 Challenge, 7-16-39—003
40-50 Champagne, 41-51-6—176
26-85 Champion, 28-31-54—433
19-29 Chance, 55-72-78—981
01-96 Chapel, 63-14-53—762
15-33 Charcoal, 18-8-14—487
27-65 Charity, 27-33-43—521
37-79 Charm, 37-64-66—366
53-56 Chase, 12-37-76—118
22-19 Cheat, 22-15-38—367
31-87 Check, 53-73-27—228
66-93 Cherry, 2-18-29—432
10-23 Chest, 14-28-35—778
01-87 Chestnut, 6-14-66—606
55-66 Chevrolet, 4-10-64—987
43-26 Chew, 50-46-76—212
19-77 Chicken, 2-11-22—343
52-56 Child, 8-19-50—919
01-14 Children, 1-12-19—219
87-50 Chimney, 26-38-44—660
32-65 Chilly, 18-36-53—863
07-09 Chin, 44-55-67-449
11-44 Chinaman, 2-8-9—7C4
33-53 Chitterlings, 49-59-6—316
78-88 Chocolate, 5-18-36—457
15-27 Choir, 13-27-55—222
22-37 Choke, 46-78-19—897
55-92 Christen, 22-27-50—912
30-03 Christmas, 15-25-35—315
8-100 Chrysler, 8-18-77—439
44-64 Church, 2-19-23—453
21-36 Cider, 18-36-54—761
05-10 Cigar, 5-10-20—112
23-25 Cigarette, 20-36-25—503
66-99 Circle, 78-76-74—002

03-42 Circumcise, 12-14-32—138
54-61 Circus, 77-57-67—221
40-70 City, 40-69-78—467
26-35 Clarinet, 4-6-16—712
02-12 Clean, 19-38-48—763
88-98 Clearing house, 8-1-7—765
15-31 Clergyman, 15-33-40—002
22-44 Clerk, 1-50-55—555
90-98 Climb, 6-11-44—616
05-40 Clinic, 19-22-37—411
06-12 Clock, 12-6-24—318
42-53 Close, 36-43-58—422
36-27 Closet, 30-27-14—516
14-73 Clothes, 43-37-28—827
61-82 Cloud, 21-8-43—916
04-08 Clover, 4-8-12—092
43-91 Clown, 14-53-67—991
18-37 Club, 27-38-45—550
22-66 Clumsy, 1-3-14—666
78-08 Coal, 5-8-40—591
34-20 Coat, 7-15-20—712
02-04 Cockeye, 37-45-55—383
27-33 Cockroach, 15-17-19—607
42-71 Cocoa, 23-44-59—551
97-99 Coffee, 78-22-70—319
01-16 Coffin, 72-68-66—499
10-25 Coin, 10-25-50—100
20-30 Cold, 20-30-39—009
14-25 Collar, 4-5-44—554
37-62 Collect, 36-18-49—687
19-76 College, 24-47-72—143
14-10 Color, 14-41-70—400
98-76 Coma, 55-66-77—912
12-22 Comb, 60-63-71—687
53-58 Combination, 2-4-6—246
01-14 Comedy, 18-43-55—123
77-81 Comet, 19-38-57—087
19-35 Comfort, 45-51-74—531
40-50 Command, 32-40-50—666
13-26 Communist, 13-39-26—113
90-99 Company, 45-55-16—154
27-47 Compel, 1-3-7—731
06-11 Complain, 19-54-77—767
44-55 Comrade, 12-44-55—541
22-28 Concert, 38-50-74—753
33-18 Confess, 4-14-53—314
01-12 Confirmation, 8-6-4—764
35-78 Confusion, 9-16-29—299

**9**

36-40 Congregation, 1-2-3—515
2-100 Congress, 26-36-48—863
48-54 Congressman, 7-12-1—117
93-87 Conquer, 53-55-63—365
11-41 Conscience, 14-4-24—566
26-90 Console, 28-38-42—232
13-49 Conspiracy, 3-13-23—234
51-62 Constipation, 19-29-9—999
83-14 Contest, 6-48-10—010
06-10 Contract, 16-10-20—415
90-97 Convention, 72-68-53—367
15-33 Convert, 18-53-12—158
12-18 Convict, 9-28-69—004
37-59 Cook, 5-10-15—765
48-78 Cool, 14-19-49—499
26-14 Copper, 66-76-78—142
58-61 Cork, 70-72-74—777
94-19 Corn, 10-16-45—065
72-87 Coronet, 12-15-31—107
02-20 Corporal, 26-10-5—125
13-18 Corpse, 53-67-13—133
90-99 Corsage, 26-51-53—562
18-33 Corset, 34-48-32—245
14-26 Costume, 19-10-8—842
29-37 Cot, 6-10-77—004
83-39 Cottage, 27-49-51—189
98-44 Cotton, 70-76-68—254
6-100 Couch, 1-3-14—111
07-11 Cough, 7-11-18—418
26-45 Count, 26-36-46—567
50-60 Countess, 44-54-66—645
11-21 Courage, 21-11-16—442
80-86 Court, 28-38-68—832
19-28 Cousin, 19-49-28—829
15-23 Cow, 6-15-66—006
07-19 Coward, 62-68-76—776
42-86 Crab, 14-27-53—321
17-24 Cradle, 8-16-71—817
07-11 Craps, 4-63-44—404
66-71 Crazy, 44-57-63—344
14-82 Crib, 8-16-71—818
37-53 Cricket, 1-7-29—515
22-90 Crime, 16-32-54—779
04-40 Cripple, 24-56-78—842
61-78 Crocodile, 1-10-39^113
20-30 Crook, 14-4-24—004
51-56 Cross, 27-54-37—512
28-74 Crow, 72-76-67—716

07-77 Crowd, 30-50-52—653
90-96 Crown, 12-42-37—341
14-44 Crucifix, 60-70-50—675
8-100 Cruel, 21-32-43—334
45-54 Crush, 54-55-61—040
16-61 Crying, baby, 11-17-3—187
24-84 Crying, man, 28-41-6—691
39-93 Crying, woman 2-4-8—549
55-63 Crystal ball, 42-18-5^114
21-12 Cuban, 9-18-47—717
59-87 Cup, 6-40-46—644
93-94 Cure, 26-46-36—014
80-28 Curls, 5-10-33—225
13-43 Curtain, 4-6-14—461
27-38 Cut, 21-56-65—256

# D

93-63 Dam, 19-37-43—339
84-97 Damage, 44-55-66—527
42-26 Damp, 12-26-58—125
03-08 Dance, 11-17-55—652
33-67 Danger, 18-31-56—892
65-95 Dark, 66-74-78—778
07-77 Daughter, 1-61-71—845
24-48 Day, 6-24-8—846
01-11 Dead, animal, 1-11-9—765
09-19 Dead, person, 9-19-2—711
13-56 Dead, relative, 3-6-5—762
83-67 Deaf, 56-76-24—423
24-44 Debt, 74-22-13—083
55-68 December, 5-14-65—606
77-14 Deep, 12-52-36—651
90-70 Defeat, 14-16-17—536
86-56 Defend, 27-9-47—742
71-97 Delay, 18-20-21—108
06-74 Demand, 62-73-56—632
14-27 Dentist, 20-30-26—223
5-100 Deny, 43-18-52—214
52-12 Desert, 28-1-22—248
47-97 DeSoto, 10-16-56—581
15-51 Destiny, 66-76-77—667
26-68 Destroy, 41-2-28—248
41-55 Detective, 34-62-71—761
82-50 Devil, 12-22-33-422
26-93 Dew, 35-18-21—312
18-45 Diamond, 2-29-73—793
52-10 Dice, 25-50-75—882
19-91 Dig, 7-26-36—723

44-66 Die, 16-44-55—503
06-56 Dime, 72-74-26—599
19-83 Dinner, 2-21-69—226
4-100 Dirt, 16-33-54—582
90-99 Disappear, 27-38-12—813
16-23 Disappoint, 3-4-11—514
28-57 Disagree, 77-78-11—177
29-89 Disaster, 8-10-14—418
16-27 Discharge, 58-68-78—778
03-33 Disease, 13-33-18—831
76-82 Disgrace, 22-38-57—753
03-09 Disguise, 16-66-76—996
80-94 Disgusted, 2-9-71—711
18-48 Dish, 1-10-19—111
10-14 Dishonest, 15-51-61—777
37-40 Disobey, 43-56-10—951
16-86 Divorce, 3-13-6—158
50-54 Dizzy, 17-11-27—006
11-21 Doctor, 5-10-25—425
66-98 Dodge, 7-11-73—586
12-15 Dog, 4-50-61—461
14-44 Doll, 68-73-43—376
55-75 Dollar, 26-46-58—842
22-82 Donkey, 29-10-4—612
73-87 Door, 70-78-76—080
07-18 Dope, 41-51-62—211
1-100 Dough, 10-20-30—231
04-06 Doughnut, 56-77-78—887
13-26 Draft, 13-33-43—344
28-40 Drag, 7-6-4—001
46-66 Dragon, 50-71-48—847
21-41 Dream, 22-12-36—632
16-34 Dress, 4-44-60—404
05-10 Drink, 2-11-13—549
87-97 Drive, 50-56-58—855
36-56 Drizzle, 37-51-66—716
20-50 Drown, 13-12-11—112
90-99 Drug, 40-44-50—145
16-39 Drum, 4-40-50—202
13-74 Drunk, man, 13-42-7—734
18-45 Drunk, woman, 8-4-2—188
01-14 Dry, 4-29-44—406
80-93 Duck, 10-16-76—711
55-60 Dumpling, 40-55-35—435
03-08 Dust, 18-78-68—881
13-55 Dying, 15-50-55-431

# E

80-90 E, 5-22-25—325
94-98 Eagle, 63-68-72—286
26-18 Ear, 5-11-55—516
78-43 Earring, 52-36-56—565
26-18 Eat, 2-21-69—269
55-76 Earthquake, 66-76-56—111
19-37 Echo, 42-53-67—044
43-51 Eclipse, 67-66-56—975
59-79 Education, 14-28-32—563
10-14 Egg, 1-3-7—002
08-16 Eight, 8-16-24—428
15-55 Elbow, 53-66-14—33f
46-14 Election, 16-55-28—855
75-83 Electricity, 29-39-54—124
24-54 Elephant, 3-10-30—412
26-59 Elevator, 5-11-55—302
31-66 Eleven, 11-22-33—321
15-78 Elope, 26-37-48—843
04-16 Embalm, 78-76-74—777
20-89 Embrace, 51-59-41—119
6-100 Empty, 6-8-14—400
44-57 Enemy, 15-72-18—171
90-92 Engaged, 52-78-62—275
03-33 Engine, 1-5-66—656
42-63 Enjoy, 14-23-50—005
12-27 Enter, 67-78-14—417
04-54 Entertain, 22-32-42—222
25-50 Entrance, 38-43-51—133
01-99 Envy, 13-33-43—301
07-10 Episcopal, 7-10-77—533
16-46 Erupt, 18-19-22—229
18-88 Escape, 14-44-10—413
37-57 Evangelist, 37-57-67—777
43-10 Evil, 1-6-76—003
20-80 Evil spirit, 61-18-64—461
73-75 Evidence, 52-57-67—556
15-55 Excuse, 27-23-31—142
14-33 Execute, 33-38-43—988
88-94 Exercise, 6-15-26—891
11-21 Explain, 51-61-71—412
40-53 Explosion, 28-39-52—232
20-30 Eye, 6-16-36—190
55-92 Eye glasses, 55-72-66—625

# F

05-09 F, 5-9-16—169
86-74 Face, 44-54-56—644
13-55 Factory, 38-15-26—613
07-14 Faint, 10-6-2—260
33-66 Fairy, 40-50-63—354
52-76 Faith, 1-7-15—571
14-33 Fall, 7-27-59—707
04-54 False, 48-58-62—264
76-36 Family, 3-6-9—876
82-93 Famous, 21-35-45—512
98-10 Fan, 10-20-78—003
56-76 Farm, 53-66-72—265
18-38 Fast, 63-52-21—423
58-62 Fat, 33-66-76—040
19-69 Father, live, 19-27-69—176
14-32 Father, dead, 1-11-19—765
56-12 Father'n-law, 44-27-5—526
22-44 Fear, 22-42-52—542
07-77 Feast, 26-37-58—789
56-93 Feather, 1-13-27—886
24-84 February, 11-18-52—119
15-99 Feel, 23-37-48—403
73-65 Feet, 2-5-39—205
04-14 Female, 18-31-14—386
42-82 Fence, metal, 21-58—623
11-18 Fence, wood, 1-11-18—178
45-58 Festival, 14-26-54—542
1-100 Fever, 26-78-68—888
38-58 Figs, 67-38-44—381
10-22 Fight, 4-18-57—718
33-54 Figure, 34-56-69—359
68-71 Filth, 3-6-9—963
50-75 Finance, 19-76-77—477
19-38 Find, 23-46-56—003
04-08 Finger, 40-50-63—684
15-23 Finish, 3-6-13—272
47-55 Fire, 6-46-69—695
07-27 Fish, 7-27-57—757
05-55 Five, 43-55-65—545
14-27 Fix, 26-36-46—236
13-48 Flag, 10-16-78—061
91-97 Flea, 70-62-76—600
16-36 Flirt, 27-44-53—582
09-89 Float, 16-76-12—412
32-86 Flood, 66-69-72—667
19-23 Floor, 19-16-13—311

91-84 Flour, 28-44-55—554
15-17 Flower, 51-49-64—379
87-99 Flunk, 58-62-36—365
14-52 Fly, 15-7-4—101
40-50 Fog, 12-17-33—277
59-69 Food, 56-69-53—365
11-21 Fool, 14-56-62—260
05-10 Foot, 8-19-28—677
81-95 Ford, 1-11-56—821
24-42 Forest, 66-74-38—187
13-27 Forget, 16-42-28—741
15-20 Fork, 1-11-20—431
04-18 Fortune, 62-70-24—426
76-81 Foul, 18-31-4—046
62-74 Four, 4-44-74—744
43-15 Fowl, 43-15-11—114
16-88 Fox, 10-11-40—385
04-16 Frame, 4-16-75—587
33-46 Fraternity, 1-3-33—331
4-100 Freak, 11-18-59—850
18-38 Freckle, 17-27-45—521
66-74 Freeze, 32-1-33—332
06-52 Friday, 13-38-49—002
70-80 Friend, 6-10 66—676
90-87 Frighten, 12-22-33—321
16-24 Frog, 16-14-3—340
53-65 Frost, 5-10-20—514
10-29 Frown, 54-57-60—655
20-40 Fruit, 10-20-49—402
07-77 Fry, 7-58-49—360
13-33 Funeral, 15-26-28—825
96-99 Fur, 44-63-74—436
8-100 Furnace, 22-53-64—812
14-48 Furniture, 4-15-20—993
18-66 Fussing, 70-72-76—277
47-58 Future, 12-14-44—441

# G

09-59 G, 9-40-57—057
94-98 Gallows, 76-72-22—113
26-36 Gamble, 54-70-63—265
10-20 Game. 9-4-6—030
13-46 Gang, 13-46-76—134
19-48 Gangster, 16-26-33—366
62-57 Garage, 5-17-27—715
29-36 Garbage, 48-56-63—354
42-58 Garden, 1-16-7—711
67-84 Garlic, 12-18-72—441

09-55 Garter, 48-55-61—771
23-29 Gas, 1-11-55—115
56-76 Gate, 26-38-75—562
04-94 General, 4-27-38—824
46-58 Germ, 18-62-41—164
16-66 Ghost, 16-26-36—666
83-94 Giant, 66-76-78—993
22-40 Gift, 6-18-12—207
19-46 Gig, 20-30-40—001
01-91 Gin, 1-5-10—879
18-48 Giraffe, 12-32-71—380
26-42 Girdle, 26-42-58—981
29-39 Girl, 29-39-41—488
16-21 Glass, 2-8-48—288
14-15 Glove, 6-10-12—146
08-88 Glow, 71-73-75—777
16-66 Go, 11-22-40—124
82-53 Goal, 44-64 52—264
05-51 Goat, 4-10-60—498
10-11 God, 10-11-20—321
62-83 Gold, 26-64-43—841
09-28 Golf, 9-18-36—669
04-44 Good luck, 4-44-7—748
57-91 Gone, 1-3-9—109
60-72 Gorilla, 18-16-72—891
65-85 Gospel, 63-53-41—413
18-26 Gossip, 16-34-48^83
05-53 Gown, 27-30-16—403
68-74 Graduate, 71-77-68—781
14-16 Grandchild, 14-16-18—114
33-18 Grandfather, 7-15-54—786
17-70 Grandmother, 1-6-7—797
12-54 Grape, 12-21-59—413
56-23 Grapefruit, 6-15-72—517
48-29 Grass, 1-3-5—005
93-86 Grasshopper, 4-9-13—333
07-13 Grave, 7-9-47—777
16-28 Gravy, 66-72-38—541
10-90 Gray, 48-58-36—040
43-58 Grease, 33-18-14—348
62-73 Greed, 13-33-39—331
55-15 Green, 55-15-25—555
01-41 Grief, 16-28-31—121
52-76 Grind, 66-78-68—876
40-50 Grocery, 18-40-46—144
07-21 Groom, 14-23-55—412
16-23 Ground hog, 4-8-12—113
55-66 Grow, 52-38-54—435

18-38 Guard, 6-18-9—169
23-43 Guest, 14-34-51—101
92-94 Guide, 62-71-70—187
21-31 Guitar, 21-31-45—278
62-89 Gun, 15-55-63—163
75-93 Gymnasium, 19-28-3—321
16-26 Gypsy, 3-8-9—993

# H

47-69 H. 9-47-69—009
51-64 Habit, 22-38-72—232
18-88 Hail, 3-13-33—303
01-16 Hair, black, 1-16-40—999
15-21 Hair, blonde, 12-21-6—565
40-60 Hair, brown, 8-11-40—761
11-91 Hair, brunette, 8-3-9—871
02-88 Hair, grey, 2-4-8—898
15-56 Hair, red, 12-16-59—117
43-45 Hairdresser, 33-44-55—895
18-26 Hall, 38-46-65—040
1-100 Halo, 1-2-3—321
05-55 Ham, 5-11-12—151
71-85 Hamburger, 25-30-49—694
14-44 Hammer, 23-44-10—114
86-93 Hammock, 66-74-14 566
15-28 Hand, 4-18-28—428
76-43 Handbag, 19-33-44—431
62-88 Handcuff, 62-72-76—776
19-37 Handkerchief, 8-9-4—496
26-18 Hang, 18-19-69—003
06-14 Happy, 17-77-21^27
23-41 Hard, 53-66-70—400
07-27 Hard luck, 7-18-45—785
90-99 Harem, 33-46-53—343
44-66 Harlem, 44-66-76—446
27-58 Harp, 12-14-44—108
14-10 Harvest, 54-56-62—265
03-08 Hash, 16-43-33—301
47-88 Hat, 15-16-40—114
19-36 Hate, 58-62-61—165
66-94 Hawaiian, 16-36-47—914
24-63 Hawk, 76-77-78—878
76-83 Hay, 13-31-43—334
19-38 H-bomb, 1-15-77—751
15-55 Head, 14-39-69—500
14-36 Headache, 16-26-45—542
29-84 Heal, 28-19-37—005
06-96 Health, 51-56-66—779

23-58 Hear, 42-53-33—090
52-66 Hearse, 22-42-54—655
14-41 Heart, 14-41-61—114
32-99 Heat, 52-67-78—888
86-15 Heaven, 1-15-55—541
20-30 Heavy, 26-27-38—826
17-77 Heel, 66-77-55—567
01-02 Hell, 1-10-3—301
25-50 Help, 25-30-50—100
38-56 Hemorrhage, 44-51-62—214
08-62 Herb, 8-21-32—228
49-69 Hero, 66-78-28—876
18-81 Hide, 9-11-14—519
33-97 High, 18-55-73—903
26-15 Hill, 42-66-40—464
07-77 Hindu, 15-28-65—610
26-33 Hit, 12-20-30—231
11-55 Hives, 56-63-10—163
87-14 Hog, 12-38-63—322
27-84 Hold, 32-66-12—123
16-33 Hold up, 24-28-36—623
55-67 Hole, 8-18-78—887
73-84 Holiday, 4-11-44—481
92-86 Home, 29-68-58—829
14-37 Hope, 41-73-75—543
55-64 Horn, 52-36-46—610
27-37 Horse, 8-10-28—651
07-21 Horse shoe, 13-31-29—777
18-32 Hose, 28-38-32—375
15-16 Hospital, 26-28-58—984
27-98 Hot, 2-16-41—402
63-21 Hotel, 60-70-77—776
26-36 House, 1-8-16—861
86-97 Humid, 13-26-47—003
15-21 Hunch, 15-21-10—111
62-38 Hungry, 26-38-48—557
93-90 Hurricane, 25-40-37—514
84-65 Hunt, 48-56-55—548
72-12 Hurt, 27-72-12—127
27-36 Husband, 6-41-50—650
19-91 Hydrant, 2-12-22—212

# I

01-11 I, 5-9-17—175
32-20 Ice, 23-2-6—622
55-65 Ice cream, 2-21-22—222
20-26 Idle, 18-62-73—318
14-54 Idol, 14-56-45—008

29-59 Image, 66-70-51—156
18-33 Imagine, 18-30-41—143
30-18 Incense, 10-14-61 116
69-80 Indian, 69-70-75—677
14-38 Indigestion, 17-29-53—152
15-55 Infant, 12-26-36—631
72-91 Infection, 28-13-30—312
01-18 Injure, 55-72-74—475
81-47 Ink, 8-14-72—817
16-36 Inquest, 51-65-18—165
53-62 Insect, 62-72-52—204
40-50 Inspect, 78-72-60—678
88-99 Installment, 16-36-28-—826
1-100 Insult, 38-41-53—313
14-44 Insurance, 20-30-36—632
76-97 Intimate, 15-20-25—512
24-46 Invalid, 60-74-38—876
39-12 Invent, 23-30-54—432
56-63 Investigate, 27-49-51—145
11-23 Invite, 19-30-36—303
10-29 Iron, 4-11-49—414
08-80 Island, 76-77-78—786
16-56 Itch, 50-30-40—000

# J

07-19 J, 7-19-57—195
51-15 Jai alai, 12-22-32—222
18-23 Jacket, 43-52-12—254
25-40 Jail, 21-46-57—249
12-27 Janitor, 2-11-21—765
06-61 January, 6-11-67—178
20-30 Jar, 10-20-30—003
78-87 Jazz, 16-8-4—408
13-26 Jealousy, 44-66-54—445
41-52 Jet, 17-18-19—181
66-88 Jew, 17-31-49—173
81-16 Jitterbug, 14-24-44—412
08-27 Job, 4-8-9—080
07-10 Jockey, 17-71-76—617
55-60 Judge, 73-18-10—113
12-34 Jug, 10-56-74—378
84-26 July, 7-17-57—701
13-23 Jump, 14-12-28—281
16-51 June, 6-15-66—505
42-87 Jungle, 68-78-12—176
19-21 Junk, 6-10-70—716
08-12 Jury, 13-15-51—111

# K

16-34 K, 38-46-63—366
53-07 Keg, 16-35-70—986
41-66 Kettle, 11-21-51—125
07-11 Key, 9-11-19—919
15-35 Kick, 63-44-50—546
13-33 Kidnap, 27-8-1—278
29-68 Kidney, 6-9-78—878
50-80 Kill, 19-49-69—660
16-96 Kindness, 53-63-73—345
36-42 Kinky hair, 27-37-72—237
30-50 Kiss, 13-23-47—762
16-28 Kitchen, 43-56-62—254
89-98 Kite, 8-9-39—040
14-52 Kitten, 70-74-24—441
57-64 Knee, 36-60-66—603
16-91 Knife, 7-43-37—689
17-73 Knock, 28-43-12—214

# L

95-15 L, 27-38-69—236
19-09 Labor Day, 19-9-69—967
87-45 Ladder, 18-27-31—178
57-91 Lady, 57-11-21—150
43-34 Lamb, 47-74-66—764
16-66 Lame, 10-6-36—661
75-96 Lamp, 6-12-20-446
17-49 Land, 53-48-21—145
36-54 Landlord, 7-17-28—568
17-53 Lantern, 70-69-9—997
49-94 Lard, 36-62-38—863
51-76 Lasso, 69-37-25—536
14-59 Laugh, 9-26-47—659
44-33 Laundry, 3-7-17—713
16-26 Law, 9-18-76—764
09-90 Lawyer, 18-38-47—381
15-57 Lazy, 66-78-14—100
22-33 Leak, 43-25-15—040
12-90 Leap, 29-49-19—942
15-52 Leap year, 3-7-8—873
14-41 Leg, 14-10-20—412
38-53 Lemon, 71-18-50—344
06-19 Lent, 71-42-33—337
3-100 Leopard, 55-57-48—225
01-06 Letter, 25-12-14—411
55-43 Lettuce, 12-44-51—210
12-26 Lice, 3-5-8—189

48-61 Lie, 53-13-48—841
33-18 Lieutenant, 6-17-27—767
57-87 Light, 78-75-15—517
16-98 Lightning, 2-12-8—128
13-27 Limp, 14-27-72—227
52-66 Linament, 66-76-16—666
30-45 Lincoln, 6-12-24—826
15-51 Lion, 61-71-68—488
62-73 Lip, 48-51-50—550
37-47 Liquid, 47-73-33—374
19-20 Liquor, 2-29-23—322
07-67 Liver, 76-70-7—777
12-82 Lizard, 21-28-12—286
26-98 Load, 43-48-57—003
44-57 Lobster, 9-11-19—909
08-78 Lock, 10-20-70—000
13-31 Locust, 46-26-16—614
56-66 Lodestone, 56-66-70—763
44-80 Log, 27-12-9—912
23-77 Look, 4-22-50—425
19-81 Lose, 56-40-71—145
27-70 Lost, 20-34-59—959
55-58 Lottery, 22-32-40—433
07-11 Love, 7-11-21—117
14-44 Lover, 32-26-43—343
27-77 Luck, bad, 57-68-74—465
37-73 Luck, good, 10-37-73—177
04-14 Lumber, 4-40-44—400
53-47 Lumbago, 14-26-34—578
16-28 Lump, 56-78-66—605
13-21 Lunatic, 42-12-14—411
67-92 Lunch, 2-69-45—410
48-53 Lye, 66-76-78—878
79-98 Lynch, 26-14-4-446

# M

33-45 M, 7-16-31—711
55-56 Machine, 10-14-29—941
78-91 Mad, 22-33-44—004
32-55 Madam, 11-31-41—111
64-27 Magic, 27-36-47—747
10-50 Magnet, 20-30-60—863
14-44 Maid, 35-65-77—705
06-19 Mail, 18-42-61—398
14-41 Man, black, 14-41-70—400
23-31 Man, white, 5-29-50—551
56-64 Man, yellow, 24-66-3—363
78-97 Manure, 4-3-1—138

4-100 Map, 12-31-64—400
17-57 Marble, 1-2-3—321
03-07 March, 44-67-32—132
28-90 Mark, 28-39-73—741
33-58 Market, 6-22-55—556
26-29 Marriage, 43-34-33—334
37-56 Mass, 18-36-56—631
11-41 Match, 1-11-40—100
19-28 Mattress, 4-8-44—484
37-81 May, 10-14-41—391
56-93 Meal, 58-68-72—275
42-58 Mean, 14-42-71—397
70-80 Measles, 70-60-40—467
93-95 Meat, 6-22-55—625
12-17 Medal, 36-12-8—816
46-64 Medicine, 28-13-9—942
33-88 Medium, 33-68-28—883
01-37 Meet, 11-69-66—169
17-71 Melancholy, 48-52-36—654
03-04 Melody, 27-37-53—332
28-33 Melon, 12-9-1—100
20-60 Memory, 39-47-57—773
54-45 Mend, 56-69-78—876
21-91 Mercy, 23-14-10—010
07-86 Mess, 77-27-17—777
12-26 Message, 20-32-44—434 .
23-31 Methodist, 7-17-49—555
28-43 Mexican, 18-43-55—476
62-66 Mice, 12-76-54—871
23-74 Midnight, 26-24-12—222
59-67 Milk, 1-45-6—456
44-54 Minister, 28-37-59—998
30-92 Mink, 14-12-4—001
96-84 Miracle, 27-38-56—652
7-100 Mirror, 69-76-66—676
36-47 Miscarriage, 21-12-3—812
21-49 Mischief, 6-16-9—966
57-84 Miser, 42-2-1—104
26-95 Miss, 28-37-58—832
32-38 Mistake, 2-6-36—662
07-47 Mistletoe, 70-50-63—357
66-69 Mistress, 14-18-37—718
13-33 Moan, 29-13-33—309
45-68 Mob, 28-45-58—848
78-97 Molasses, 27-72-76—672
42-56 Mole, 44-48-12—214
27-99 Monday, 31-50-72—810
18-44 Money, big, 18-44-61—899

08-28 Money, little, 8-10-28—102
10-20 Money, green, 5-10-2—790
11-55 Monkey, 5-11-55—818
77-93 Monument, 29-33-41—139
23-34 Moon, full, 13-69-70—706
46-72 Moon, new, 46-60-72—967
57-86 Mop, 44-57-23—375
40-90 Morgue, 8-17-29—928
15-25 Mortgage, 25-52-75—555
48-78 Mosquito, 4-11-33—314
17-63 Moss, 29-9-19—912
04-14 Modi, 54-68-75—565
22-70 Mother, live, 22-69-7—764
12-27 Mother, dead, 2-7-9—761
03-09 Mother'n-law, 3-6-9—369
26-74 Motor, 40-50-77—755
15-29 Motorboat, 29-14-33—511
44-68 Motorcycle, 4-20-68—111
55-78 Mountain, 21-38-36—632
26-13 Mourning, 24-34-42—442
44-81 Mouse, 11-76-57—877
22-49 Mouth, 29-38-62—239
07-14 Move, 18-19-20—953
32-56 Mud, 7-10-77—789
26-64 Mule, 27-52-73—761
11-51 Mumps, 6-8-10—106
92-88 Murder, 2-12-22—698
46-67 Muscle, 18-8-78—888
21-89 Mushroom, 20-54-62—265
06-16 Music, 8-18-28—897
52-44 Mustache, 17-27-7—127

# N

68-76 N, 27-73-72—723
12-27 Nag, 29-27-25—002
04-08 Nail, 4-6-8—864
16-55 Naked, child, 16-17-5—175
11-74 Naked, man, 11-56-7—373
03-38 Naked, woman 3-15-6—818
09-90 Name, 48-69-71—471
46-53 Navy, 25-30-40—500
27-87 Neck, 3-6-22—226
19-43 Necklace, 15-52-33—335
52-87 Needle, 42-56-37—754
36-94 Negro, 4-41-72—664
55-26 Neighbor, 70-76-47—777
03-17 Nephew, 14-27-19—121
22-36 Nervous, 7-15-36—617

48-98 Nest, 18-42-44—408
18-29 Net, 10-11-22—212
33-55 News, 22-33-55—523
42-58 Newspaper, 9-10-14—911
96-46 New Year, 1-11-21—111
30-03 Nickel, 5-10-30—315
41-53 Niece, 8-27-33—237
27-96 Night, 16-27-18—612
42-77 Nightmare, 4-19-38—889
09-99 Nine, 9-49-59—999
26-43 Noise, 66-73-75—576
13-17 Nose, 7-11-77—132
01-14 Nosebleed, 27-44-14—114
24-87 Notice, 37-77-74-473
44-63 November, 5-37-66—102
05-15 Novena, 14-42-10—104
19-91 Nude, child, 16-27-55—175
11-24 Nude, man, 11-56-74—373
33-46 Nude, woman, 3-15-4—818
14-44 Numb, 52-13-33—335
58-93 Number, 4-8-28—812
57-66 Nun, 27-37-56—603
47-52 Nurse, 20-15-12—252
33-68 Nursing, 18-36-44—438
76-94 Nut, 9-19-50—915

# O

14-28 O, 19-21-56—125
31-40 Ocean, 25-52-27—725
7-100 October, 6-11-16—223
18-39 Octopus, 8-16-32—218
90-94 Odor, 14-6-11—106
23-37 Offer, 12-18-33—002
27-56 Office, 44-72-39—934
37-82 Officer, 50-60-30—365
15-30 Oil, 4-44-67—159
38-96 Ointment, 24-29-35—532
73-78 Old, 27-8-58—800
82-12 Oldsmobile, 2-11-22—538
14-17 Olive, 14-23-38—004
09-18 Omen, 38-51-53—355
44-54 One, 7-11-61—161
27-88 Onion, 33-63-48—777
90-47 Opera, 40-69-70—407
36-63 Operation, 12-6-3—361
88-78 Opium, 28-33-43—332
43-70 Orange, 22-32-42—418
15-62 Orchestra, 2-1-22—364

07-70 Orchid, 17-71-76—677
60-98 Organ, 48-18-28—412
53-62 Orient, 23-62-53—352
44-66 Orphan, 13-31-39—931
21-58 Overcoat, 4-41-44—912
19-37 Owl, 27-14-42—200
43-35 Oyster, 17-37-67—678

# P

15-54 P, 3-20-28—113
78-86 Packard, 24-44-53—352
23-42 Pail, 27-38-43—337
19-24 Pain, 4-6-15—154
30-40 Paint, 2-12-22—243
06-16 Pal, 27-38-10—100
22-59 Pan, 5-11-15—515
7-100 Pancake, 29-57-62—252
09-19 Pants, 14-4-1—104
48-66 Paper, 11-52-73—573
22-45 Parade, 53-72-78—875
76-91 Paradise, 14-7-4—471
70-80 Paralyze, 41-51-56—655
52-96 Parchment, 19-37-39—93⌐
94-98 Park, 6-16-66—006
10-20 Parole, 18-37-42—584
14-54 Parrot, 23-32-38—832
87-78 Partner, 17-13-30—317
93-42 Party, 66-77-22—002
20-54 Past, 43-40-20—244
19-91 Pastor, 16-66-77—766
46-52 Paw, 8-18-4—418
35-40 Pay, 14-7-77—707
26-31 Payday, 36-38-47—743
14-07 Peace, 21-57-61-161
26-34 Peach, 26-36-68—416
45-93 Peacock, 7-9-14—497
67-74 Peanut, 22-30-40—432
27-37 Pear, 38-16-42—212
15-34 Pearl, 18-68-76—671
26-13 Peddler, 43-47-74—444
52-76 Pen, 1-11-38—998
18-98 Pencil, 16-21-7—721
01-99 Penny, 1-16-61—832
86-91 Pension, 30-50-70—735
14-51 Pentecostal. 8-10-31—622
07-16 People. 14-21-33—301
24-58 Pepper, 15-56-42—251
66-71 Perfume, 50-55-60—850

14-15 Perjury, 48-56-16- 654
18-39 Persecute, 12-17-18—811
04-54 Person, 23-32-28—882
26-96 Perspire, 6-8-12—266
52-68 Pest, 17-42-57—701
37-42 Pet, 29-38-45—543
59-61 Petticoat, 72-74-64—467
41-52 Pew, 18-36-44—430
37-70 Phonograph, 33-78-4—547
56-84 Photograph, 2-6-11—162
30-55 Piano, 4-10-67—321
14-29 Pick, 11-14-38—148
44-57 Pickle, 1-11-69—127
33-93 Picnic, 33-66-22—263
18-38 Picture, 10-12-55—711
04-41 Pie, 10-29-39—334
52-58 Pig, 2-11-18—321
16-66 Pigtail, 18-36-16—611
46-24 Pigeon, 24-74-78—877
57-97 Pile, 12-24-56—652
03-14 Piles, 13-27-37—721
44-91 Pill, 54-21-11—112
23-32 Pillow, 23-64-72—886
55-59 Pimple, 14-23-37—737
60-71 Pin, 6-16-32—206
90-96 Pinch, 52-67-36—652
22-49 Pink, 14-28-68—881
01-16 Pint, 7-12-44—002
17-27 Pipe, 1-5-11—101
90-76 Pistol, 7-20-57—867
54-65 Pitcher, 15-25-51—125
33-66 Pity, 42-78-66—646
12-87 Place, 19-33-42—584
53-39 Plan, 15-62-77- 761
27-30 Planet, 27-38-39—978
63-78 Plant, 10-16-44—106
42-57 Plate, 48-62-70—706
18-88 Play, 7-9-11—791
14-44 Plow, 4-7-16—761
5-100 Plumber, 24-70-74—472
57-75 Plymouth, 3-10-58—094
13-30 Pneumonia, 53-57-59—955
45-58 Pocket, 5-10-78—781
06-77 Poetry, 26-66-37—736
19-33 Poison, 7-9-10—109
93-63 Poker, 4-29-44—318
88-42 Pole, 7-15-76—212
35-40 Police, 28-35-67-818

22-32 Policy, 4-14-45—478
06-08 Politician, 50-60-78—857
26-15 Pomade, 22-33-54—432
78-92 Pontiac, 8-11-22—538
66-78 Pony, 14-42-48—444
43-93 Pool, 5-66-77—983
12-27 Poor, 36-16-46—631
10-20 Pop, 18-37-49—002
74-89 Porch, 44-52-50—554
43-80 Pork, 8-14-74-418
27-42 Porter, 11-22-39—921
07-19 Postman, 56-16-26—665
56-78 Post office, 1-7-12—217
40-99 Pot, 10-19-27—112
21-93 Potato, 21-15-39—768
57-62 Powder, 14-36-18—007
28-82 Power, 26-32-36—633
52-57 Pray, 31-52-57—881
27-37 Preacher, 30-37-57—663
38-47 Pregnant, 11-21-31—111
26-96 Prejudice, 18-66-71—618
14-29 Presbyterian, 6-8-48—226
38-64 Present, 28-37-44—432
52-37 President, 69-70-42—418
78-91 Pretend, 42-48-56—465
40-50 Pretty, 48-12-14—040
89-99 Price, 18-16-11—118
56-62 Priest, 56-62-26—665
37-93 Prince, 18-36-6—055
86-89 Princess, 1-3-9—933
29-14 Print, 2-5-69—269
20-80 Prison, 20-40-60—000
15-28 Prisoner, 15-13-14—451
67-71 Prize, 66-76-77—767
24-44 Prizefighter, 8-16-36—618
06-09 Problem, 24-38-58—824
18-39 Profane, 17-35-42—247
56-67 Professor, 16-19-21—211
50-75 Profit, 55-64-73—365
26-46 Promise, 18-14-4—448
58-62 Proof, 58-66-72—807
49-42 Property, 51-33-27—735
03-33 Prophecy, 23-31-38—831
54-86 Proposal, 54-62-64—465
27-36 Prosecute, 40-17-10—174
25-80 Prosperity, 55-56-57—555
27-33 Prostitute, 27-33-22—237
58-76 Protection, 4-5-8—571

21-38 Protest, 16-45-76—674
42-55 Provide, 7-16-20—207
14-22 Prunes, 41-44-53—441
37-23 Psalm, 23-11-77—727
56-94 Puddle, 16-13-33—661
20-40 Pull, 1-22-50—250
05-55 Pumpkin, 5-19-55—317
15-23 Punch, 66-42-10—146
76-84 Punish, 9-18-37—900
14-23 Puppet, 16-24-38—831
97-48 Puppy, 17-44-55—006
23-41 Purple, 23-41-44—242
32-82 Purse, 17-77-78—877
12-24 Pusey, white, 12-24-3—564
48-58 Pusey, black, 48-58-6—546
19-26 Push, 16-60-70—001
43-82 Puzzle, 47-20-36—624

# Q

89-91 Q, 1-12-60—601
44-88 Quarantine, 48-56-66—465
12-06 Quarrel, 72-74-75—577
56-27 Quart, 16-32-48—841
05-10 Quarter, 20-30-40—478
88-96 Queen, 57-67-77—776
1-100 Queer, 14-2-3—302
55-75 Question, 64-32-16—616
12-14 Quiet, 12-18-4—481
66-73 Quit, 26-6-42—526

# R

16-32 R, 16-28-43—124
07-14 Rabbit, 44-50-62—189
55-94 Raccoon, 7-1-11—481
37-46 Race, 12-14-52—987
12-42 Race horse, 53-46-25—546
16-55 Racket, 6-26-34—004
03-42 Radio, 7-11-36—790
19-88 Rag, 44-56-69—956
53-72 Raid, 1-8-18—930
61-12 Railroad, 4-11-44—134
02-22 Rain, 2-22-43—237
19-58 Rainbow, 13-45-70—724
54-62 Raincoat, 29-53-18—815
80-90 Raise, 20-30-51—105
12-42 Raisins, 12-44-59—154
16-66 Rape, 16-27-33—273
74-85 Rash, 56-72-18—817

56-22 Rat, 14-41-59—668
33-51 Rattle, 3-2-1—134
66-99 Rattlesnake, 46-16-6—689
08-18, Razor, 7-11-77—372
17-37 Read, 9-10-14—961
9-100 Rebel, 43-47-56—654
87-91 Receive, 29-33-71—173
44-56 Recognize, 32-23-60—623
02-07 Record, 58-61-77—765
18-88 Rectum, 18-66-36—636
01-91 Red, 19-50-72—185
33-68 Referee, 29-48-54—454
27-29 Refuse, 16-37-50—531
33-94 Regret, 47-57-67—774
20-46 Reindeer, 5-12-62—738
58-83 Relative, 56-78-76—659
24-36 Relief, 27-38-44—438
18-88 Religion, 18-61-65—615
29-43 Remember, 43-57-69—936
07-16 Rent, 14-26-42—796
21-42 Repair, 40-13-16—114
67-85 Rescue, 7-15-55—517
80-66 Resemble, 45-19-17—714
51-90 Resist, 29-38-74—473
27-36 Respect, 20-30-66—632
14-28 Rest, 19-8-41—007
43-22 Restaurant, 24-42-56—654
06-56 Return, 66-77-44—476
37-49 Reveal, 23-31-17—711
56-65 Revenge, 19-76-62—291
23-32 Reverend, 17-19-29—997
48-67 Reward, 6-14-29—904
16-61 Rheumatism, 56-71-6—575
18-39 Ribbon, 14-12-11—114
42-68 Ribs, 63-13-33—303
77-99 Rice, 70-74-76—677
50-75 Rich, 45-56-60—454
74-51 Riddle, 64-73-76—767
28-78 Ride, 4-44-50—445
22-45 Rifle, 22-36-45—542
36-19 Ring, 9-11-20—920
58-78 Riot, 44-54-74—444
10-12 Rip, 21-10-4—412
32-58 Ritual, 14-32-66—632
50-61 River, 55-62-77—776
19-39 Roach, 1-2-3—322
26-57 Road, 11-27-37—716
33-77 Roast, 7-14-28—364

17-18 Rob, 29-33-35—509
23-56 Robber, 56-61-66—666
39-27 Robe, 9-11-31—139
52-78 Robin, 66-70-44—447
16-49 Rock, 51-69-70—481
74-87 Romance, 71-70-68—867
12-19 Roof, 27-34-43—302
15-04 Room, 48-59-78—895
45-26 Root, 24-33-39—293
91-16 Rope, 1-11-61—117
62-39 Rosary, 39-48-58—889
51-58 Rose, 6-16-62—433
40-52 Rough, 16-7-47—006
36-91 Round, 8-48-60—648
70-86 Row, 24-37-19—090
15-72 Rub, 16-66-71—161
33-47 Rubber, 33-38-64—433
04-15 Rug, 29-56-74—427
12-17 Rum, 61-58-31—160
51-01 Run, 51-10-2—215
94-49 Rupture, 13-33-46—643
23-58 Rush, 75-77-64—475

# S

36-66 S. 19-38-57—135
07-12 Sabbath, 7-14-41—117
14-34 Sacrifice, 29-38-41—438
63-91 Sacrilege, 1-3-9—983
72-78 Sad, 24-31-42—206
12-16 Saddle, 12-16-26—621
11-44 Safe, 18-39-54-459
44-53 Sail, 27-33-74—477
30-61 Saint, 30-40-55—333
07-79 Sale, 66-69-77—761
15-17 Saloon, 23-14-44—552
31-23 Salt, 16-7-15—000
14-35 Sand, 19-37-52—271
41-59 Sandwich, 64-78-74—446
65-76 Satan, 13-33-63—331
84-94 Saturday, 21-15-68—202
06-90 Save, 14-55-73—385
52-85 Savings, 27-38-56—653
33-44 Savior, 33-44-48—844
12-22 Saw, 4-10-50—145
01-06 Sawdust, 27-6-4—407
15-41 Saxophone, 12-28-41—374
54-16 Scald, 16-54-68—722
19-58 Scale, 19-39-78—938

23-12 Scandal, 26-53-72—125
06-14 Scar, 7-15-33—317
77-94 Scare, 18-33-46—604
21-85 Scarf, 4-27-44-404
52-63 Scheme, 15-38-41—131
14-26 School, 11-40-66—146
01-19 School mate, 22-40-2—241
29-58 Scissors, 18-38-49—931
42-90 Scold, 24-52-42—245
16-29 Score, 1-6-12—211
88-63 Scratch, 19-34-40—434
27-42 Scream, 55-61-72—276
50-64 Screw, 49-12-8—849
23-38 Scripture, 23-38-56—658
66-73 Scrub, 28-38-50—235
24-27 Sea, 7-11-17—222
74-82 Seal, 11-19-30—417
50-60 Seance, 42-33-58—833
31-44 Search, 26-14-34—416
76-82 Seat, 8-17-31—101
15-33 Secret, 29-48-53—354
06-12 Seduce, 67-74-70—746
17-87 See, 1-14-53—311
13-30 Seed, 44-48-60—466
18-49 Seize, 18-36-48—863
56-61 Self, 40-58-14 444
74-14 Sell, 26-14-8—800
55-64 Send, 22-19-56—779
09-88 September, 21-39-58—632
22-32 Sermon, 23-48-22—223
16-27 Servant, 64-56-68—864
07-77 Seven, 7-17-27—777
16-56 Sew, 4-11-44—401
19-50 Sex, 19-40-50—500
10-25 Sex organ, 10-50-20—251
36-84 Shadow, 33-49-54-454
59-71 Shampoo, 66-78-63—386
16-44 Shake, 5-55-71—505
19-56 Shape, 23-12-7—712
77-83 Shave, 1-11-14—114
42-56 Shawl, 18-9-14—419
70-17 Sheep, 8-18-55—189
24-33 Shell, 29-48-53—358
04-41 Shelter, 27-48-56—654
23-62 Shepherd, 33-36-48—843
05-53 Sheriff, 70-64-76—676
29-42 Shine, 18-6-16—608
76-64 Shingle, 4-14-40—140

19-49 Ship, 22-33-11—231
23-36 Shipwreck, 47-57-78—882
70-72 Shirt, 12-15-48—114
14-57 Shock, 28-46-60—682
07-11 Shoe, 5-9-16—201
07-77 Shoemaker, 57-77-64—467
15-36 Shoot, 7-11-58—659
36-60 Shoulder, 33-23-13—322
19-49 Shovel, 16-64-58—778
04-93 Show, 1-33-66—366
12-27 Shy, 18-46-54—400
14-58 Sick, 10-20-30—876
34-44 Side, 76-72-64—467
56-63 Sign, 16-23-38-482
74-58 Signal, 56-63-37—733
86-97 Silence, 29-34-76—673
12-28 Silk, 27-48-53—002
25-50 Silver, 51-55-62—265
16-73 Sin, 17-29-75—577
27-18 Sing, 8-18-4—814
14-43 Sink, 48-53-12—205
62-79 Siren, 16-12-4—412
22-50 Sister, 22-26-50—632
29-62 Sister'n-law, 19-37-68—863
06-66 Six, 6-16-66—661
18-48 Skate, 11-15-54—154
7-100 Skeleton, 14-3-1—341
60-75 Skin, 26-18-13—316
18-30 Skinny, 4-15-39—685
43-67 Skirt, 10-39-57—310
89-91 Skull, 29-49-59—999
10-20 Sky, bright, 10-16-40—165
03-12 Sky, dark, 14-61-53—114
64-73 Slander, 29-33-45—543
32-46 Slap, 20-40-60—000
58-77 Slave, 4-17-21—471
96-14 Sleep, 14-28-56—414
82-30 Sleet, 4-14-44—404
12-56 Sleigh, 12-17-31—113
09-18 Slice, 74-52-7—774
26-34 Slide, 11-18-54—185
22-46 Slip, 22-16-66—662
78-90 Slippers, 14-20-7—274
20-41 Sliver, 1-3-4—436
53-62 Slop, 3-11-33—303
03-44 Slow, 24-55-18—008
9-100 Slug, 26-62-48—584
12-20 Small, 36-46-59—954

47-56 Smallpox, 12-76^78—87⁻
16-45 Smart, 6-9-18—819
27-48 Smash, 27-49-74—477
66-84 Smear, 18-33-44—438
22-96 Smell, 1-12-19—191
43-07 Smile, 26-6C-63—366
58-99 Smog, 42-58-69—016
23-32 Smoke, 3-12-63—316
14-20 Snail, 8-11-14—418
88-96 Snake, 16-34-64—895
13-48 Snake bite, 19-39-27—59
22-34 Sneak, 22-34-43—344
10-66 Sneeze, 14-27-64—682
23-48 Snob, 43-29-77—772
52-67 Snore, 23-14-8—804
39-74 Snow, 14-45-70—186
82-19 Snowball, 12-18-71—147
01-16 Soap, 26-39-58—853
22-14 Sober, 20-30-38—833
64-83 Sock, 22-37-14—413
27-19 Soft, 16-7-2—271
37-45 Soldier, 37-77-64—466
23-27 Son, 23-27-29—992
63-49 Son'n-law, 4-7-9—974
07-76 Song, 28-36-38—829
14-22 Sore, 20-34-44—444
66-83 Sorrow, 16-12-10—121
95-42 Sorry, 56-68-71—175
61-78 Soul, 23-32-14—432
29-42 Sound, 22-39-40—493
66-99 Soup, 54-43-76—764
18-33 Sour, 12-8-6—602
04-41 Spanish, 1-15-45—369
46-53 Spareribs, 27-38-41—141
32-49 Speak, 55-43-58—555
50-60 Spend, 19-21-33—832
08-66 Spider, 11-21-32—231
73-84 Spiderweb, 8-12-46—688
23-78 Spill, 44-52-58—855
42-69 Spin, 21-10-4-100
58-94 Spinach, 11-39-48—134
90-83 Spirit, 16-66-75—577
42-09 Spittoon, 3-10-33—318
19-91 Splash, 6-62-76—666
83-38 Splinter, 12-52-44—441
64-72 Split, 15-7-19—710
12-82 Spoon, 3-7-45—375
17-34 Sport, 36-61-69—966

23-48 Spot, 24-33-20—200
62-74 Sprain, 37-66-19—916
69-14 Spray, 20-30-40—000
52-68 Spring, 17-27-36—632
27-39 Sprinkle, 48-54-52—255
48-54 Spy, 78-74-70—707
66-89 Squeeze, 61-63-73—376
44-73 Squirrel, 34-71-48—378
13-48 Stab, 14-23-58—852
56-94 Stable, 55-53-50— 535
62-87 Stage, 19-38-59—998
48-52 Stagger, 27-34-43—343
16-60 Stain, 12-22-15—516
29-42 Stairs, 20-30-40—403
07-85 Stale, 55-64-70—765
56-79 Stallion, 29-33-37—733
23-32 Stamp, 44-56-63—365
29-86 Stand, 15-55-47—745
48-57 Starch, 36-12-10—112
67-87 Stare, 60-70-74—477
12-24 Stars, few, 12-19-23—114
68-74 Stars, many, 69-70-71—775
14-42 Starve, 29-33-48—843
29-38 State, 66-72-58—508
56-69 Statue, 27-36-23—322
28-38 Steal, 8-16-29—600
49-56 Steam, 33-47-74—347
68-73 Steel, 54-43-27—724
89-99 Steep, 68-17-12—211
07-43 Steer, 19-39-76—760
28-47 Step, 23-32-62—263
56-23 Stepchild, 56-23-33—333
78-80 Stepfather, 76-78-68—867
93-14 Stepmother, 21-31-40—432
42-51 Stick, 24-37-70—007
6-100 Stiff, 45-54-63—365
67-12 Still, 12-8-4—482
06-18 Sting, 1-3-5—501
27-36 Stir, 22-27-36—637
38-54 Stocking, 7-29-77—707
67-83 Stock market, 1-6-3—268
76-62 Stomach, 64-70-36—646
40-53 Stone, 26-34-39—933
28-67 Stop, 18-12-4—428
32-46 Store, 23-37-48—001
88-73 Storm, 16-12-39—939
14-40 Story, 66-73-75—576
53-68 Stove, 5-9-45—940

72-47 Strain, 30-42-56—664
59-68 Strange, 44-58-63—365
15-20 Stranger, 21-33-48—843
18-88 Strangle, 12-7-17—717
10-21 Straw, 38-14-6—606
17-20 Strawberry, 1-7-20—172
56-63 Stream, 31-46-58—854
72-84 Street, 39-45-72—901
66-79 Strength, 68-72-34—433
53-92 Strike, 12-14-3—341
03-83 String, 28-32-47—061
76-79 Stroke, 56-65-58—856
10-12 Strong, 32-31-29—929
33-48 Struggle, 18-20-44-428
20-40 Stubborn, 56-12-39—931
38-59 Student, 6-8-10—186
64-76 Stupid, 44-53-22—252
91-93 Subpoena, 70-28-64—468
06-16 Substitute, 12-14-16—611
27-39 Success, 7-11-21—217
47-64 Sue, 12-47-59—951
22-32 Sugar, 23-50-77—775
08-65 Suicide, 8-65-70—707
29-92 Suit, 14-39-63-401
38-46 Summer, 29-36-16—669
54-71 Summons, 44-54-71—175
12-20 Sun, 39-78-52—408
13-43 Sunburn, 1-22-41—682
05-10 Sunday, 5-10-40—140
17-29 Sunstroke, 42-68-31—316
38-45 Supper, 21-69-53—216
68-77 Support, 64-13-59—953
43-21 Surgery, 32-60-36—662
15-62 Surprise, 23-43-69—964
74-93 Suspicion, 2-70 74—477
58-22 Swallow, 14-33-37—731
07-16 Swamp, 61-71-58—857
23-32 Swear, 71-76-67—766
29-57 Sweat, 24-44-62—002
55-90 Sweep, 15-34-38—834
76-73 Sweet, 1-7-11—171
42-51 Sweetheart, 45-72-63—734
17-39 Swell, 3-35-39—933
43-34 Swim, 7-9-11—791
90-94 Swindle, 25-73-62—267
12-42 Swing, 4-36-64—463
17-77 Sword, 1-7-57—175
07-70 Sympathy, 46-65-74—476

# T

60-69 T, 60-69-75—607
90-60 Table, 5-66-75—298
33-48 Tack, 26-40-53—354
16-74 Tail, 74-76-66—666
25-50 Tailor, 6-37-67—376
56-79 Take, 16-41-61—164
60-32 Talent, 47-75-68—367
04-44 Talk, 27-29-38—876
72-84 Tall, 48-53-12—215
29-31 Tambourine, 29-39-5—761
40-64 Tantrum, 76-42-21—124
11-17 Tap, 17-38-78—007
39-56 Tape, 7-77-20—277
62-74 Target, 39-69-9—999
21-31 Taste, 27-49-21—200
47-57 Tattoo, 70-50-30—357
68-43 Tax. 78 18-43—348
11-91 Tea, 15-56-78—157
40-50 Teacher, 31-78-55—731
39-58 Team, 50-1-44—415
26-84 Tear, 19-40-22—869
34-42 Tears, 8-71-64—467
16-28 Tease, 28-45-78—874
39-42 Teeth, 3-10-33—329
74-93 Telegram, 51-72-60—275
16-80 Telephone, 2-41-46—442
40-32 Television, 20-23-30—238
01-16 Tell, 73-77-27—777
78-32 Temper, 42-74-34—437
19-56 Temple, 9-29-52—959
27-24 Temptation, 30-3-47—334
10-30 Ten, 48-24-10—100
72-83 Tenant, 10-53-25—553
10-31 Tender, 54-4-43—445
61-73 Tennis, 11-31-21—232
18-51 Terrible, 75-44-45—407
41-60 Terror, 5-50-30—355
72-57 Test, 22-26-38—836
32-93 Testament, 12-55-74—475
92-34 Testify, 32-76-62—267
11-91 Thanks, 44-50-6—504
50-59 Thanksgiving, 5-6-7—165
02-42 Theater, 6-45-66—543
62-74 Thick, 51-27-37—737
12-33 Thief, 13-23-48—842
21-49 Thigh, 46-77-60—674

90-43 Thin, 33-52-53—332
21-12 Think, 57-7-17—007
34-40 Thirst, 24-28-39—489
13-75 Thirteen, 47-78-65—567
03-89 Thorn, 53-59-41—149
35-43 Thoroughbred, 14-34-56—653
33-58 Thread, 58-25-62—26?
52-79 Threat, 8-48-51—158
13-24 Three, 1-54-72—274
64-76 Thrill, 15-29-76—519
77-57 Throat, 35-2-18—825
05-88 Throb, 59-30-63—363
65-94 Throne, 9-49-54—499
25-81 Throw, 36-30-40—430
44-78 Thumb, 26-50-61—165
53-95 Thunder, 16-60-55—661
08-14 Thursday, 1-11-60—555
66-76 Tickle, 61-31-55—356
27-39 Tie, 3-6-22—226
36-99 Tiger, 48-57-66—654
67-86 Tight, 27-51-74—451
07-79 Time, 37-62-33—367
54-37 Tip, 10-31-56—310
45-57 Tired, 17-52-32—357
15-81 Tissue, 7-11-17—717
20-33 Toast, 63-28-32—328
16-96 Toad, 53-57-33—337
37-85 Tobacco, 1-8-15—185
08-18 Toe, 64-68-22—228
46-68 Toilet, 18-38-54—581
55-82 Tomato, 12-23-28—122
97-42 Tombstone, 65-55-44 445
28-84 Tongue, 11-33-40—341
38-69 Tongue-tied, 19-58-6—689
17-98 Tonsil, 29-34-59—392
83-86 Tooth, 11-20-56—250
47-99 Toothache, 39-66-74—961
56-72 Top, 12-56-60—665
30-70 Torch, 30-34-59—203
71-93 Torpedo, 20-57-68—867
48-24 Touch, 40-67-35—428
8-100 Toupee, 21-58-60—586
10-63 Towel, 10-12-29—101
51-76 Tower, 2-43-63—618
21-10 Town, 33-64-72—423
92-45 Toy, 9-29-60—926
11-19 Track, 12-38-42—400
01-93 Traffic, 48-20-76—334

46-70 Tragedy, 21-37-49—682
38-57 Train, 15-45-63—393
77-92 Traitor, 65-74-60—482
64-72 Tramp, 34-44-51—533
11-94 Trance, 22-8-19—607
20-43 Transfer, 49-3-64—812
41-71 Trap, 26-34-43—234
27-47 Trash, 11-45-74—512
52-78 Travel, 1-7-36—595
28-42 Traveler, 29-33-35—683
21-82 Treason, 23-66-77—392
12-91 Treasure, 6-8-11—412
02-65 Treat, 50-30-20—629
39-95 Tree, 6-11-44—616
12-58 Tremble, 35-42-18—998
28-79 Trial, 67-46-65—546
48-43 Tribe, 16-7-19—002
22-40 Trip, 12-31-54—667
53-44 Triplets, 1-10-12—298
29-72 Trombone, 29-31-44—808
13-49 Trouble, 47-63-76—612
18-83 Trousers, 4-8-36—974
37-97 Trout, 66-43-20 246
66-70 Truant, 24-51-37—735
20-30 Truck, 12-18-45—222
29-96 Trumpet, 12-25-31—117
41-59 Trunk, 68-48-78—708
54-80 Trust, 17-37-52—257
67-73 Truth, 67-78-74—477
30-96 Try, 10-32-49—003
03-60 Tub, 11-16-39—684
90-84 Tuberculosis, 53-69-7—519
18-39 Tuesday, 4-14-60—791
55-81 Tumble, 2-29-70—270
42-97 Tumor, 13-50-68—345
74-86 Tune, 25-33-49—943
68-50 Tunnel, 5-54-7—800
14-16 Turban, 38-42-23—343
43-95 Turkey, 23-41-70—023
31-85 Turn, 70-51-67—216
26-61 Turnip, 49-56-73—278
25-75 Turtle, 14-69-34—439
82-28 Twelve, 1-8-9—991
15-43 Twins, 52-67-70—684
32-51 Twist, 39-55-71—572
04-69 Twitch, 26-34-7—436
62-86 Two, 17-29-52—587
98-76 Typewriter, 15-70-64-—671

56-83 Typhoon, 12-21-40—210

# U

44-33 U, 11-14-39—131
57-93 Ugly, 53-63-73—355
11-77 Ukelele, 12-18-40—666
84-52 Ulcer, 56-72-60—725
30-63 Umbrella, 10-18-66—106
12-14 Umpire, 54-48-34—543
70-99 Uncle, 47-39-59—473
58-85 Unconscious, 7-40-51—514
34-41 Uncover, 16-35-71—173
16-87 Under, 55-70-12—570
45-64 Underwear, 4-38-44—639
31-86 Undress, 57-73-6—437
45-78 Unfair, 24-39-12—219
05-08 Uniform, 18-36-56—863
35-53 Unite, 48-50-69—906
13-29 Untie, 27-58-33—335
23-46 Union, 13-33-63—133
71-87 Upside down, 4-7-5—574
22-65 Upstairs, 9-22-72—279
06-36 Urge, 37-44-24—420
14-54 Urinate, 2-59-16—165
32-79 Use, 57-63-77—707

# V

37-88 V, 10-15-44—101
7-100 Vacant, 28-42-58—248
47-59 Vaccinate, 23-38-66—326
17-88 Valentine, 4-11-63—416
46-66 Valley, 17-73-34—437
23-38 Vanish, 5-24-57—572
33-72 Vase, 20-30-42—003
15-47 Vaudeville, 19-43-60—641
01-24 Veal, 10-29-46—169
34-07 Vegetable, 29-75-25—257
39-67 Veil, 39-59-74—749
24-48 Vein, 18-33-44—444
60-89 Verdict, 3-13-21—231
73-55 Verse, 61-26-67—676
18-60 Vest, 13-40-52—541
16-25 Veteran, 48-50-61—654
35-67 Vibration, 30-44-38—834
61-40 Vice, 76-60-40—460
08-80 Vicious, 20-33-51—532
49-90 Victor, 45-66-70—764
34-40 Victory, 4-45-62—452

02-26 Village, 19-27-39—971
19-74 Vinegar, 41-61-75—466
56-89 Violet, 5-6-10—560
25-68 Violin, 7-9-11—791
44-54 Virgin, 31-77-62—371
36-91 Virus, 63-24-7—066
50-62 Vision, 14-46-56—564
17-27 Visit, 20-28-31—281
09-81 Voice, 78-42-63—334
62-75 Volcano, 21-6-8—862
20-69 Vomit, 47-52-63—526
37-18 Voodoo, 32-62-41—463
39-57 Vote, 6-64-59—586
16-64 Vow, 34-50-27—782
03-96 Voyage, 10-54-66—763
30-76 Vulture, 20-22-49—983

# W

26-86 W, 15-26-69—569
57-22 Wagon, 4-8-44—484
43-72 Wait, 29-53-59—607
65-99 Wake, 65-31-73—357
51-49 Walk, 2-11-22—212
05-10 Wall, 24-33-60—615
16-40 Wallet, 78-74-72—741
77-82 Walnut, 2-30-36—230
28-58 Waltz, 28-52-66—123
49-64 Wander, 19-35-45—398
87-91 Want, 51-59-71—004
17-66 War, 4-16-41—461
62-74 Warden, 66-72-60—986
41-97 Warm, 23-30-74—548
16-23 Warning, 12-13-15—964
91-95 Warrant, 27-29-47—812
31-88 Wart, 48-58-62—500
27-38 Wash, 8-9-14—814
47-50 Washington, 4-8-9—528
53-64 Watch, 71-76-22—934
67-78 Watchman, 50-67-47—672
59-65 Water, cold, 45-56-32—732
11-14 Water, hot, 8-11-14—789
37-56 Water, muddy, 1-3-7—653
29-47 Waterfall, 9-39-47—322
42-89 Watermelon, 11-14-1—111
15-39 Wave, 49-68-77—888
50-98 Weak, 7-17-27—404
7-100 Wealth, 18-36-47—981
76-84 Wear, 14-41-51—630

33-42 Weary, 2-26-30—964
68-79 Weather, 70-60-40—272
16-03 Weave, 12-48-52—961
60-75 Web, 35-46-67—894
32-38 Wedding, 22-30-32—032
49-56 Wedding cake, 3-7-8—482
12-24 Wednesday, 10-20-30—187
80-91 Weed, 15-27-34—796
07-14 Week, 37-39-56—045
31-42 Weep, 18-19-37—422
43-69 Weight, 47-57-65—293
64-23 Welcome, 4-68-74—684
99-87 Well, 69-21-32—017
75-51 Wet, 61-70-65—863
20-34 Whale, 9-39-47—937
61-90 Wheel, 17-40-19—541
15-17 Whip, 13-38-40—767
38-59 Whiskers, 7-8-9—987
81-92 Whiskey, 15-45-49—972
15-70 Whisper, 29-4-30—348
55-66 Whistle, 46-37-67—522
33-62 White, 20-30-44—123
24-13 Wicked, 25-67-70—764
26-34 Widow, 39-56-62—178
28-37 Wife, 8-24-59—911
21-10 Wig, 44-63-42—763
63-78 Wild, 27-30-49—376
34-53 Will, 5-33-51—421
52-91 Win, 21-40-62—788
18-82 Wind, 71-45-58—158
10-14 Window, 4-8-48—484
71-60 Wine, 5-10-45—504
44-59 Wings, 3-28-66—866
29-64 Wink, 71-41-51—745
32-48 Winner, 25-61-73—263
60-53 Winter, 14-32-42—142
11-01 Wipe, 1-40-15—105
83-95 Wire, 61-52-54—526
35-42 Wisdom, 22-62-37—237
44-54 Wish, 31-70-75—307
18-20 Witch, 9-60-77—767
64-79 Witness, 41-30-20—541
45-72 Wolf, 29-39-59—471
65-14 Woman, black, 6-4-9—890
02-27 Woman, white, 2-7-5—876
44-53 Woman, yellow, 1-3-4—640
24-92 Wood, 18-77-69—555
66-79 Woods, 59-26-35—265

54-62 Wool, 15-76-61—117
46-35 Word, 42-4-43—324
27-24 Work, 63-64-71—176
13-66 Workman, 23-58-75—582
61-73 Worm, 39-50-57—559
93-95 Worry, 27-37-72—689
36-67 Worse, 27-29-31—339
12-19 Worship, 43-64-68—468
84-88 Wreath, 38-45-55—854
22-49 Wreck, 16-44-48-000
55-67 Wrist, 57-75-65—576
17-02 Wristwatch, 74-32-12—213
74-86 Write, 35-54-75—754
15-20 Wrong, 17-19-38—269

# X

76-84 X, 6-13-43—614

# Y

24-38 Y, 1-8-25—258
19-91 Yacht, 27-18-49—110
47-85 Yankee, 48-31-42—241
62-94 Yard, 54-65-68—886
25-38 Yawn, 17-56-76—003
12-37 Year, 28-39-55—228
56-14 Yell, 8-73-68—863
75-89 Yellow, 24-45-6—442
18-20 Young, 55-61-77—765

# Z

56-95 Z, 3-19-27—312
15-51 Zebra, 12-30-50—755
48-12 Zodiac, 48-37-42—243
48-63 Zoo, 55-72-66—756

"A GOOD NAME is rather to be chosen than great riches,
and loving favour rather than silver and gold."
Prov. 22:1

"Let us speak plain: there is MORE FORCE in NAMES
Than most men DREAM of."
Lowell

"The invisible thing called a GOOD NAME is made up of
the breath of NUMBERS that speak well of you."
Lord Halifax

## A

10-52 Aaron, 12-17-48—114
24-16 Abadia, 5-27-34—426
06-10 Abagail, 9-18-36—508
51-34 Abana, 16-37-59—610
42-66 Abbey, 49-28-55—326
33-93 Abbie, 41-54-62—778
11-84 Abbot, 14-29-53—386
64-15 Abbott, 1-11-21—521
18-41 Abby, 13-41-76—816
69-89 Abdi, 44-56-14—502
50-83 Abe, 38-58-27—129
25-32 Abel, 13-47-74—147
11-49 Abelardo, 19-66-42—249
49-70 Abernathv, 13-17-32—716
17-88 Abigail, 2-12-24--421
19-65 Ables, 51-62-77—765
01-87 Ableton, 9-17-39—919
31-40 Abner, 14-39-71—584
48-29 Abraham, 2-67-76—267
12-86 Abram, 4-12-18—814
30-67 Abrams, 2-9-15—643
04-07 Abrego, 44-54-62—205
68-99 Absalom, 9-10-18—809
56-71 Achiles, 56-10-4—005
47-63 Acisclo, 3-13-42—241
13-20 Acislo, 12-16-66—890
90-85 Ackerson, 4-14-44—312
31-02 Ackley, 12-16-52—816
18-62 Acosta, 33-48-52—166
30-66 Ada, 7-2-59—323
39-46 Adair, 8-15-43—245
72-69 Adaline, 9-18-43—481
14-82 Adam, 1-10-56—156
100-8 Adams, 46-36-73—214

21-53 Adamson, 7-11-77—263
64-92 Adan, 3-10-11—113
32-84 Adapearl, 19-48-56—541
70-08 Addie, 48-15-36—604
81-85 Addison, 5-14-67—723
29-61 Addy, 4-12-15—514
19-45 Adean, 23-31-54-4-32
22-98 Adeil, 77-11-59—813
67-73 Adela, 43-53-62—556
24-83 Adelaide, 32-16-49—507
54-20 Adelardo, 65-71-77—777
84-60 Adelbert, 21-35-72—104
71-86 Adele, 5-22-34—452
05-15 Adelgaster, 44-55-66—600
21-91 Adelia, 31-15-72—214
74-97 Adeline, 4-13-50—504
38-72 Adell, 38-66-75—753
55-80 Adelson, 31-3-49—572
09-59 Adene, 32-45-67—002
73-82 Adis, 6-24-56—966
58-44 Adlene, 8-44-62—330
15-50 Adline, 21-52-68—651
48-89 Adolf, 42-64-71—106
35-23 Adolfo, 7-30-72—237
63-94 Adolph, 29-51-19—915
85-90 Adolphes, 5-18-65—712
43-65 Adolphus, 28-34-62—256
36-77 Adoración, 20-50-60—000
22-62 Adria, 8-41-71—748
26-35 Adrian, 30-62-50—311
40-76 Adrien, 4-30-60—712
16-47 Adrienne, 75-63-26—667
39-91 Affonso, 28-40-50—500
95-64 Agatha, 1-8-16—116
26-86 Agins, 19-49-70—991
61-74 Agnes, 6-7-8—800
25-75 Agnew, 32-68-48—595
34-18 Agud, 27-39-62—232
46-51 Aguerrí, 9-62-44—469
06-92 Aguila, 38-42-70—040
24-57 Aguilar, 48-61-16—446
52-60 Aguiluz, 1-18-78—787
75-96 Agustin, 42-63-72—264
37-42 Ahart, 12-37-48^-08
45-87 Aida, 26-69-75—576
12-69 Aiken, 10-60-40—317
33-76 Aikens, 5-27-35—555
36-41 Aileen, 47-52-56—427

53-59 Aimee, 17-36-63—007
03-10 Akers, 2-22-69—372
38-78 Akins, 35-48-58—843
27-93 Alabama, 12-17-32—308
74-19 Alan, 11-14-17—111
54-75 Alana, 25-38-42—583
16-25 Alane, 59-60-63—365
58-82 Alayza, 12-73-75—419
97-11 Alba, 77-29-47—702
77-79 Alban, 46-29-12—121
44-26 Albergarius, 7-9-14—197
16-29 Albert, 11-19-21—891
68-80 Alberta, 4-18-69—290
55-88 Albertha, 34-48-56—345
28-94 Albertia, 16-19-78—989
13-42 Albertine, 58-62-28—472
50-57 Alberts, 17-44-78—308
27-48 Albertson, 1-12-29—356
37-98 Albright, 5-7-15—382
41-56 Albritton, 8-44-49—454
04-78 Albuquerques, 1-3-19—910
95-59 Alcacovas, 68-74-66—666
57-81 Alcala, 74-76-77—764
17-77 Alcalde, 15-27-42—247
42-99 Alcantara, 12-43-56—541
28-38 Alcides, 33-57-69—963
79-96 Alda, 57-66-18—008
14-43 Aldrich, 76-27-38—830
22-23 Alejandro, 24-36-42—240
10-85 Alejo, 19-23-41—121
57-89 Alelia, 8-18-38—532
06-16 Aleman, 38-43-67—186
19-56 Aleñe, 4-27-61—247
33-48 Aletha, 8-18-54—452
28-72 Alethea, 56-63-76—604
55-62 Alethia, 63-70-73—377
20-21 Alex, 12-40-50—004
48-67 Alexander, 11-22-33—123
91-71 Alexandra, 15-49-72—111
54-57 Alexia, 64-72-86—417
78-93 Alexis, 1-47-65—564
20-25 Alfaro, 28-40-34—432
70-78 Alfonsina, 21-33-44—443
63-53 Alfonso, 16-26-31—122
35-49 Alfred, 17-22-31—213
57-86 Alfreda, 27-34-43—524
22-33 Alfredo, 2-12-8—001
01-09 Alfreds, 18-35-4—222

17-19 Algernon, 10-48-57—754
64-69 Aliatar, 66-69-16—611
19-38 Alice, 8-16-42—416
42-52 Alicee, 5-7-12—510
38-51 Alicia, 34-47-74—774
11-87 Alida, 22-49-51—154
68-76 Alie, 67-72-27—207
36-42 Aline, 9-19-69—910
78-64 Alisa, 3-35-45—553
19-81 Alison, 50-68-10—001
23-14 Alla, 11-14-73—702
34-43 Allan, 16-18-24—411
15-51 Allean, 11-69-70—009
29-82 Allegra, 23-32-46—223
33-67 Allen, 3-10-27—568
18-78 Allende, 36-56-66—634
12-88 Allene, 12-14-38—809
46-72 Alley, 24-51-58—552
50-61 Allie, 56-77-52—324
02-14 Allinia, 14-65-39—387
89-93 Allison, 50-10-60—232
37-48 Allyne, 2-13-37—360
21-49 Alma, 3-33-52—816
38-66 Almedia, 25-37-43—347
12-16 Almeta, 7-17-42—658
10-07 Almira, 52-66-41—145
30-38 Almiranta, 4-37-50—007
09-90 Alonso, 13-9-18—819
82-17 Alonza, 26-53-64—462
14-28 Alonzo, 23-10-77—668
65-70 Alorence, 1-3-8—999
10-08 Aloysius, 38-54-28—853
19-91 Alphenia, 14-16-76—664
24-48 Alphonse, 8-38-48—842
39-41 Alphonso, 44-56-78—332
17-77 Alphra, 17-47-77—774
13-31 Alston, 18-70-78—570
7-100 Alta, 16-23-33—302
47-57 Alter, 78-68-50—678
21-73 Alteros, 20-30-41—129
38-84 Altes, 46-62-53—347
56-27 Althea, 9-17-64—567
16-19 Altie, 32-19-33—163
83-34 Alton, 4-11-14—870
42-56 Alva, 34-44-56—653
39-92 Alvar, 45-53-62—259
05-58 Alvares, 19-61-39—960
12-81 Alvarez, 12-51-61—112

34-43 Alvaro, 31-77-43—003
26-82 Alvaroz, 24-12-36—621
08-18 Alvenia, 40-50-62—400
16-29 Alverna, 8-24-58—346
33-48 Alvero, 44-60-48—833
27-45 Alvin, 10-17-68—223
19-39 Alvina, 18-37-41—171
15-93 Alvins, 9-31-55^5E
47-74 Alvita, 47-74-76—677
81-25 Alvonia, 30-76-38—870
09-18 Alwin, 10-17-68—171
26-04 Alyssa, 43-16-37—040
59-94 Alzena, 17-59-39—997
42-15 Amabel, 1-4-74—445
41-69 Amabelle, 7-42-31—137
28-75 Amado, 29-36-43—343
32-60 Amalia, 10-20-35—521
46-53 Amanda, 9-42-30—302
76-87 Amander, 58-75-64—768
24-95 Amaraes, 66-76-16—666
61-77 Amateau, 6-14-34—617
56-42 Amate, 16-41-63—562
20-30 Amaya, 76-67-56—203
14-46 Amazon, 28-37-46—162
48-57 Amber, 57-67-77—567
44-78 Amberose, 10-52-61—447
24-93 Ambrose, 1-11-27—117
57-62 Ambrosio, 40-50-20—000
43-96 Ameldia, 21-73-69—527
79-90 Amelia, 6-14-66—918
24-33 Amenta, 72-62-53—367
14-92 America, 5-56-16—616
31-80 Americo, 15-30-45—538
52-62 Americus, 1-12-40—113
78-63 Amerson, 39-43-36—333
19-97 Ames, 12-21-40—819
01-03 Ammie, 5-11-77—501
23-42 Amois, 27-37-47—777
64-46 Amorita, 64-46-34—344
40-12 Amos, 8-24-60—826
86-99 Amparo, 55-74-18—229
23-07 Ampuero, 23-43-62—072
47-51 Amy, 4-8-54—845
10-12 Ana, 12-21-65—869
33-55 Anastasia, 24-37-63—353
69-74 Anatol, 65-30-74—693
26-38 Anatole, 5-1-47—321
54-89 Anderson, 44-54-34—161

40-43 Andia, 36-29-40—009
04-77 Andre, 51-64-77—045
97-79 Andrea, 11-2-46—620
16-20 Andres, 23-64-73—233
22-53 Andreu, 15-35-53—315
01-68 Andrew, 8-20-72—729
12-15 Andrews, 31-43-62—121
88-96 Andy, 50-31-48—986
32-39 Aneita, 4-66-39—324
42-64 Angel, 3-28-42—223
09-15 Angela, 10-49-51—154
67-91 Angelester, 34-65-67—663
14-25 Angelica, 63-74-25—146
76-82 Angelina, 27-46-76—762
19-02 Angeline, 17-45-78—780
52-68 Angelle, 48-63-68—524
27-87 Angelo, 4-27-78—878
11-21 Angie, 22-33-74—042
44-66 Angeleter, 48-66-73—36±
39-75 Angus, 16-67-75—776
14-41 Anibal, 32-63-41—141
27-14 Anice, 2-9-7—812
03-30 Aniceto, 26-49-60—030
27-51 Anise, 32-62-75—365
41-95 Anita, 12-14-37—505
13-33 Ann, 47-58-61—133
21-72 Anna, 12-21-65—869
48-18 Annabel, 62-48-18—148
27-72 Annabele, 31-46-72—27±
16-86 Annabell, 21-68-76—68E
12-24 Annabelle, 1-5-33—123
21-65 Anne, 12-21-65—869
31-74 Anneberg, 31-40-59—71±
11-63 Annette, 9-5-11—302
13-93 Annice, 6-25-34—933
24-65 Annie, 12-21-65—869
40-65 Anniston, 1-39-40—390
50-37 Ansley, 35-67-73—735
18-29 Ansurez, 20-69-78—202
10-05 Anthony, 10-13-21—321
65-85 Antoinette, 45-50-7—85
34-94 Anton, 70-7-34—004
43-34 Antonia, 6-24-36—632
17-73 Antonio, 5-10-20—102
18-49 Antony, 10-13-21—321
45-54 Applin, 61-37-68—454
04-40 April, 44-8-51—080
47-94 Arabella, 19-77-78—947

27-83 Arabelle, 12-21-65—869
64-91 Aragon, 23-52-64—916
48-18 Araujos, 25-52-72—481
37-16 Araya, 39-45-61—167
46-96 Arboleda, 5-10-49—287
22-62 Arbuckle, 30-69-72—190
18-48 Arch, 12-18-59—174
41-78 Archer, 22-41-39—811
03-08 Archibald, 4-33-43—342
67-98 Archie, 5-15-67—657
61-16 Arcineaga, 53-71-61—161
24-31 Arcola, 3-10-60—403
10-24 Arcos, 38-16-24—108
47-90 Ardella, 14-44-60—040
23-34 Ardenie, 54-59-43—333
38-60 Ardessa, 3-17-60—387
56-78 Ardie, 72-78-68—888
12-14 Arelia, 5-11-16—602
71-84 Arellano, 19-36-71—874
60-30 Arenzana, 26-60-30—006
59-75 Arevalo, 58-47-75—579
01-41 Argentino, 55-71-73—011
36-46 Argie, 12-8-56—701
79-94 Arias, 13-43-73—339
37-51 Aris, 73-51-37—735
04-44 Aristides, 9-18-44—489
29-92 Arizcun, 42-56-65—554
36-58 Arizona, 27-15-45—370
13-91 Arjibay, 40-57-69—973
19-99 Arjona, 2-19-39—991
25-45 Arkel, 56-70-45—457
11-44 Arlean, 27-41-44—442
16-22 Arlenathy, 19-56-61—162
40-80 Arlene, 5-14-63—769
57-75 Arietta, 15-32-45—718
02-12 Arline, 41-53-64—022
31-36 Armand, 28-57-67—772
81-76 Armas, 20-76-78—872
53-89 Armenia, 8-40-53—839
12-70 Armenta, 58-70-42—258
44-66 Armette, 21-46-52—242
26-55 Armetto, 15-26-35—553
17-92 Armond, 55-28-57—917
23-48 Armstead, 30-48-23—343
39-22 Armstrong, 2-11-22—110
30-56 Arnaldo, 17-59-74—056
65-82 Amelie, 12-21-65—221
35-92 Amester, 39-35-33—333

12-16 Ameta, 42-54-62—216
74-93 Arnett, 2-10-12—514
21-17 Arnetta, 69-71-21—119
16-71 Arnold, 3-16-71—932
83-42 Amulfo, 7-75-42—248
18-63 Arolus, 60-53-63—186
25-32 Arrieta, 29-49-25—223
04-07 Arrington, 18-22-7—774
53-84 Arroyo, 43-38-53—333
28-37 Arsnell, 76-70-37—287
53-48 Arsular, 9-15-56—405
27-38 Arteaga, 57-44-33—345
15-69 Artemio, 15-37-69—369
72-86 Arthur, 1-16-36—146
23-59 Artie, 56-49-61—665
18-36 Artise, 72-74-68—778
10-90 Arturo, 17-27-37—213
24-33 Asa, 41-58-33—243
12-26 Asbell, 9-71-62—002
19-39 Ashby, 14-41-33—123
27-56 Ashcraft, 15-50-56—312
64-73 Asher, 56-64-73—675
87-99 Ashford, 22-70-78—998
17-33 Ashley, 12-45-67—903
24-40 Ashstone, 35-18-6—802
68-73 Ashton, 67-59-62—861
29-36 Ashworth, 21-29-36—322
10-12 Asken, 8-55-66—101
87-94 Askew, 13-30-40—004
08-12 Aston, 3-8-50—212
44-67 Asuncion, 42-44-67—444
58-74 Asur, 69-73-74—779
16-29 Atanasio, 20-54-61—204
13-46 Ateman, 11-35-76—075
77-94 Athaides, 22-58-45-471
22-86 Atkins, 11-17-56—480
32-57 Atkinson, 19-27-47—237
45-63 Attie, 45-54-63—164
69-84 Atwood, 14-43-69—869
11-23 Aubrey, 22-46-68—112
19-47 Aubry, 11-39-58—812
29-31 Audie, 19-29-31—193
56-94 Audrey, 1-12-51—907
27-18 Augie, 44-72-18—787
76-82 August, 7-31-59—317
39-95 Augusta, 73-38-65—563
57-63 Augustin, 16-21-47—647
48-78 Augustine, 5-9-45—812

24-39 Augusto, 38-41-70—070
33-66 Augustus, 19-36-49—949
30-70 Aureliano, 60-70-30—000
96-98 Aurelio, 2-45-48—984
24-49 Aurlyne, 32-49-64—444
11-17 Aurora, 77-17-27—654
25-36 Austin, 18-34-63—362
24-59 Austing, 27-59-68—987
78-87 Auterbery, 17-61-78—118
19-30 Autry, 9-11-30—618
11-13 Ava, 21-13-7—137
50-79 Avary, 46-74-50—507
17-71 Avelino, 6-17-71—116
08-12 Avery, 8-12-42—218
25-40 Avila, 62-68-75—045
6-100 Avis, 6-16-10—166
60-74 Axel, 18-33-74—743
06-66 Azalee, 6-15-66—913
45-54 Azalia, 53-54-56—553

# B

22-93 Babe, 16-68-22—286
16-66 Babette, 14-41-60—272
85-17 Babo, 17-37-45—902
36-74 Bacellares, 4-13-62—232
55-68 Bacon, 9-19-29—805
66-81 Bacot, 40-66-69—640
22-35 Baden, 12-18-40—169
67-84 Badford, 5-67-76—678
29-92 Badger, 29-39-52—992
31-54 Badillo, 51-67-54—315
44-66 Baharens, 23-64-66—263
18-75 Bailey, 12-18-37—8C8
16-61 Baird, 48-50-60—004
54-69 Bait, 38-66-69—356
65-83 Baity, 15-78-65—567
42-38 Baker, 10-18-11—360
57-71 Baldomcro, 50-57-71—175
23-53 Baldridge, 4-37-53—333
21-44 Baldwin, 13-30-44—818
11-30 Balentine, 8-11-49—272
74-91 Balin, 65-77-68—876
37-57 Ball, 44-39-15—195
22-64 Ballard, 10-39-37—833
29-38 Ballentine, 24-49-54—445
26-35 Baltasar, 36-50-60—300
52-25 Baltazar, 28-50-52—300
77-36 Baltimore, 3-10-53—780

43-92 Baldwin, 32-56-73—333
15-63 Bamore, 11-15-17—111
80-90 Bandy, 48-70-65—574
12-28 Bangs, 3-13-33—382
37-73 Baniak, 25-35-73—723
05-15 Banks, 5-15-19—742
35-81 Banna, 13-37-59—606
37-51 Banning, 5-11-37—573
22-99 Banta, 25-36-39—390
27-42 Baquedano, 76-42-27—276
89-62 Baquero, 64-62-18—661
37-48 Barbara, 18-42-21—212
25-36 Barber, 25-36-39—390
16-24 Barbett, 13-19-47—429
39-59 Barbitt, 34-47-59—954
25-36 Barbour, 8-36-74—144
84-92 Barbudas, 20-30-55—005
19-98 Barcena, 26-19-17—161
27-34 Barco, 54-62-66-411
34-46 Barders, 10-24-36—624
20-80 Barkens, 32-17-54—235
72-88 Barker, 15-37-68—986
37-41 Barkley, 27-75 37—318
61-82 Barkus, 1-10-41—514
26-62 Barlow, 37-39-71—443
43-78 Barner, 63-43-22—112
74-27 Barnes, 18-27-50—579
03-07 Barnett, 3-7-11—444
78-87 Barnetta, 4-8-12—841
42-56 Barney, 42-49-56-457
23-32 Bamhardt, 23-38-34—744
53-49 Baron, 4-21-49—878
64-86 Barr, 67-78-64—460
10-12 Barre, 32-12-10—002
57-83 Barren, 54-57-68—573
25-54 Barrientos, 39-54-73—482
24-19 Barrio, 14-77-64 444
17-56 Barris, 34-53-56—613
85-71 Barron, 23-31-71—113
58-75 Barros, 1-33-66—576
35-05 Barrott, 52-66-21—653
42-97 Barrow, 8-12-21—177
55-33 Barry, 43-33-55—535
28-43 Bartelsa, 3441-56—101
96-84 Barthelemy, 65-76-69—967
16-56 Bartholomew, 448-9—392
26-65 Bartol, 42-26-65—562
56-38 Bartolomé, 6-18-34—412

38-11 Bartolomeo, 6-18-34—412
75-95 Barton, 48-22-57—907
34-43 Basham, 244143—343
88-08 Basil, 51-64-78—876
76-92 Baskin, 23-14-71—482
43-57 Baso, 9-2243—243
18-83 Bass, 8-11-18—311
14-04 Basso, 9-22-14—041
35-94 Batebond, 5-23-35—532
02-12 Bates, 2-12-21—806
27-38 Batie, 40-38-27—728
58-66 Battle, 13-63-66—865
38-49 Battles, 16-1949—111
12-82 Baugh, 25-50-75—570
27-47 Baum, 39-56-74—300
33-93 Bautista, 13-52-26—357
27-36 Baxter, 1-10-40—231
13-43 Bayliss, 3448-74—759
26-84 Baylock, 26-64-74—464
67-36 Baylor, 63-67-69—696
29-33 Baynes, 4-29-39—320
18-59 Baz, 21-31-41—181
44-51 Bazo, 26-33-51—134
29-92 Beal, 62-29-34—422
18-81 Bean, 18-28-38—888
03-16 Beard, 12-16-24-426
24-67 Beartha, 74-37-22—273
20-37 Beasley, 18-27-37—020
04-14 Beatrice, 4-14-18—184
19-90 Beatrix, 49-39-29—991
20-34 Beatriz, 19-61-34—431
15-45 Beauchamp, 7-7345—155
04-08 Beaufort, 4-8-45—369
41-73 Beaulah, 16-69-73—341
78-52 Beavers, 45-55-52—555
90-31 Beck, 3040-60—000
63-40 Becker, 18-2940—433
10-48 Beckett, 1048-72—500
39-93 Beckham, 3944-22-483
59-09 Bedelía, 65-59-72—942
51-72 Bedell, 44-56-72—275
62-81 Bedford, 3-29-62—263
12-24 Bee, 15-24-12—225
35-40 Beecher, 29-35-56—406
42-98 Beeks, 22-2842—222
15-50 Bejas, 57-50-15—157
30-70 Belinda, 10-70-60—007
21-71 Belisario, 21-34-71—111

23-37 BeU, 8-11-27—573
29-77 Bella, 18-20-29—927
01-81 Bellamy, 2-3-1—012
49-61 Bellany, 21-58-61—168
24-53 Belle, 7-6-53—677
39-89 Beltran, 12-41-62—175
12-14 Ben, 12-41-62—175
05-50 Benambores, 5-10-50—787
15-70 Benard, 4-15-46—708
17-77 Bender, 2-17-77—396
12-22 Bendix, 6-10-20—203
36-39 Benedict, 11-44-59-407
25-76 Benedicta, 2-7-9—907
03-30 Benedictine, 3-11-30—309
48-29 Benes, 20-71-48—290
13-36 Benetta, 13-30-36—363
88-07 Benigno, 9-34-46—693
38-43 Benita, 16-60-62—162
56-79 Benito, 56-69-70—079
29-99 Benjamin, 31-51-55—315
18-21 Bennett, 10-30-52—456
56-69 Bennie, 31-51-55—315
35-47 Bennitt, 17-35-56—357
56-69 Benny, 31-51-55—315
27-38 Benson, 15-18-59—381
49-60 Bentaker, 36-46-49—518
45-92 Bentley, 28-45-50—320
28-32 Benton, 32-53-49—840
43-75 Berkeley, 9-43-75—874
68-29 Berman, 13-45-59—354
13-47 Bernabe, 59-60-61—567
20-80 Bernadette, 8-37-47—747
46-64 Bernadine, 47-64-46—646
43-82 Bernal, 72-74-68—877
20-88 Bernard, 5-14-16—546
43-73 Bernardino, 47-73-38—002
06-10 Bernardo, 38-48-53—623
53-78 Bemett, 7-10-78—743
29-47 Bemette, 60-47-77—647
19-91 Bernice, 8-19-23—230
40-57 Bernie, 9-61-40—474
23-51 Berry, 20-38-23—002
07-77 Bert, 19-7-47—077
26-32 Berta, 17-3-45^451
17-45 Bertha, 17-3-45—451
39-56 Berthia, 8-60-37—956
41-62 Bertram, 15-41-62—562
22-76 Berwick, 59-19-76—229

07-87 Berwin, 5-19-45—710
17-70 Beryl, 36-46-70—347
24-42 Bessie, 41-31-74—262
52-16 Bessy, 31-6-16—616
13-31 Best, 18-35-31—851
43-72 Bethea, 14-58-72—275
38-66 Betsy, 21-53-38—638
31-69 Bettie, 62-45-69—136
19-50 Betts, 5-34-50—019
64-66 Betty, 42-54-66—904
64-66 Bettye, 42-54-66—904
25-34 Beulah, 19-25-47—195
14-56 Beverley, 57-22-14—514
37-57 Beverly, 28-33-37—732
25-75 Bey, 18-22-25—500
04-90 Bianca, 1-64-9—049
43-39 Bibbins, 16-52-43—394
34-52 Bibbs, 18-34-52—368
12-18 Bieford, 56-44-18—214
15-30 Bigbee, 63-23-30—003
77-47 Bigges, 37-27-77—665
21-34 Bill, 23-19-64—732
24-42 Billie, 3-7-12—271
23-64 Billy, 23-19-64—732
10-14 Billye, 14-37-38—332
88-99 Binford, 10-32-28—889
19-38 Bingham. 26-35-48—344
17-74 Binnie, 4-43-74—174
07-11 Birdie, 7-11-59—921
22-09 Birtie, 5-9-55—818
06-60 Bishop, 5-10-60—883
16-36 Bissell, 15-23-36—864
03-83 Bivens, 4-55-33—330
24-41 Bixie, 37-41-62—145
23-59 Black, 31-59-62—212
17-37 Blackman, 17-37-78—313
21-33 Blackstone, 12-21-33—322
38-98 Blackwell, 12-27-45—431
27-57 Blaine, 27-57-72—717
52-29 Blair, 12-16-19—109
26-74 Blake, 19-38-74—383
16-42 Blakeley, 5-16-42—245
11-32 Blanch, 11-32-69—906
09-69 Blanche, 11-32-69—906
44-84 Blanco, 33-44-42—844
23-48 Bland, 15-48-63—404
91-12 Blankney, 65-17-12—917
27-96 Blanks, 42-72-27—272

39-89 Blanton, 10-39-2—564
02-12 Blas, 21-41-52—022
45-82 Blasco, 3-45-11—311
60-95 Blocker, 30-54-60—953
15-50 Blossom, 15-50-34—523
26-38 Blount, 38-26-50—562
14-21 Blout, 14-19-27—802
16-46 Blue, 13-40-46—643
20-49 Blumenthal, 7-71-27—879
34-94 Blunt, 20-53-34—943
28-14 Blyden, 28-14-69—654
44-88 Board, 29-70-48—480
08-71 Bob, 39-52-71—087
53-66 Bobbie, 7-11-16—666
45-66 Bobby, 7-11-16—666
12-81 Bodley, 78-8-26—817
53-38 Bolanos, 51-15-53—353
39-58 Bolden, 11-39-58—837
12-33 Boldridge, 1-39-48—841
68-15 Bolds, 28-38-68—688
58-70 Boles, 12-50-58—705
82-63 Boling, 69-40-36—639
01-10 Bolton, 1-6-9—407
13-93 Boman, 49-68-52—254
44-80 Bomar, 77-25-44-480
25-60 Bond, 2-27-37—605
21-67 Bone, 48-24-67—762
87-93 Bohomme, 67-14-10—879
42-46 Boniface, 15-18-70—587
54-71 Bonita, 36-2-54—177
12-28 Bonnice, 26-47-68—121
20-30 Bonnie, 76-41-60—203
11-45 Booker, 7-11-45—769
52-79 Boone, 9-32-49—999
72-83 Booth, 46-13-3—368
10-20 Bopau, 11-66-75—600
05-15 Borcosque, 3-9-12—512
43-73 Borden, 10-28-43—373
26-86 Borris, 3-33-8—886
34-42 Boseman, 25-45-42—425
19-28 Boss, 1-19-28—213
14-57 Boston, 39-57-26—714
61-37 Bottoms, 15-50-61—337
15-55 Bougliny, 35-31-55—531
22-34 Bounie, 44-12-34—424
06-78 Bowden, 26-3-50—050
12-34 Bowen, 19-30-65—392
15-92 Bowers, 43-74-76—673

57-97 Bowie, 11-29-57—797
14-35 Bowles, 41-27-35—817
30-50 Bowman, 17-37-59—305
56-97 Bowser, 73-51-56—659
06-73 Boyce, 34-16-6—670
49-85 Boyd, 6-30-49—058
08-18 Boyden, 11-18-45—509
79-40 Boykins, 4-10-40—308
47-86 Braddock, 44-47-57—378
21-39 Bradford, 10-12-39—612
23-43 Bradley, 23-42-71—604
52-94 Bradshaw, 12-27-52—898
19-68 Brady, 3-6-19—718
74-80 Eragancos, 1-18-74—740
29-33 Bragas, 27-37-63—339
77-85 Braggs, 11-77-78—704
12-42 Branch, 12-14-62—261
10-31 Brandon, 13-31-44—187
98-68 Braner, 36-47-68—698
64-82 Branicic, 9-26-64—826
61-93 Branner, 46-14-61—931
16-90 Brant, 54-71-61—167
35-73 Brantley, 2-35-15—325
43-68 Bratton, 16-4-37—684
33-66 Braulio, 19-45-66—336
02-12 Braxton, 22-23-68—612
17-24 Bray, 17-39-62—805
24-33 Braylock, 25-64-33—304
32-48 Brenda, 8-55-28—80
84-71 Brent, 15-3-16—841
41-92 Brewer, 41-55-71—448
48-76 Brewster, 9-15-78—701
26-38 Brian, 26-38-35—308
7-100 Brice, 7-31-47—377
57-99 Bridge, 28-57-72—275
19-09 Bridges, 8-11-29—518
11-20 Bridget, 11-17-20—702
12-24 Briggs, 3-10-48—224
13-33 Brigham, 77-45-33-762
29-92 Bright, 48-17-38—929
50-75 Brigido, 14-65-75—055
27-20 Brigit, 38-21-27—217
16-53 Brim, 56-60-61—165
61-62 Brimm, 22-29-61—121
14-16 Brinkley, 4-14-46—782
27-38 Britt, 49-2-27—223
69-45 Britton, 51-45-69—567
14-74 Broacher, 73-62-74—771

33-82 Broadman, 30-39-33—383
57-75 Brodie, 50-18-57—755
07-15 Brock, 3-14-15—158
42-12 Brombly, 20-12-42—124
19-99 Bronner, 57-66-69—961
41-34 Bronson, 3-41-56—103
36-39 Brook, 1-31-36—393
39-91 Brooker, 5-19-39—133
10-91 Brooks, 6-10-41—487
18-67 Brooms, 54-67-22—001
42-76 Browder, 32-40-63—762
18-58 Brown, 18-39-68—481
23-53 Browne, 25-39-53—85
46-52 Browning, 13-27-36—524
27-38 Brownlee, 27-38-49—856
65-70 Broxton, 62-65-70—070
52-10 Broyles, 19-38-52—370
23-35 Bruce, 2-60-35-401
28-82 Brumfield, 17-12-28—221
78-64 Bruner, 64-78-73—372
12-21 Brunetti, 12-21-27—490
15-87 Bruno, 12-56-74—432
49-42 Brunson, 17-27-49—555
03-13 Bruntley, 3-11-35—808
29-56 Bryan, 11-34-48—390
33-27 Bryant, 12-27-33—101
55-73 Bryson, 34-11-55—155
29-95 Buchanan, 6-14-66—616
72-27 Buckley, 44-61-26—727
04-44 Buckner, 32-44-49—550
37-33 Bue, 10-33-53—375
65-60 Buelah, 3-70-78—007
13-71 Buell, 24-43-71—173
9-100 Buenaventura, 9-19-3—990
22-49 Bueno, 77-10-22—492
38-81 Bufant, 32-60-25—605
25-52 Buffet, 25-43-67—303
16-56 Bufford, 7-19-56—407
56-88 Buford, 8-12-34—534
40-14 Buie, 23-69-72—142
36-63 Bulah, 7-76-35—363
24-76 Buler, 42-5-44—762
01-11 Bulea, 11-31-9—111
22-39 Bullard, 2-10-22—509
05-06 Bullock, 1-5-6—777
83-96 Bumstead, 29-48-18—903
64-43 Bundy, 59-24-43—649
10-30 Bunnie, 20-68-73—382

27-59 Burch, 41-8-59—279
37-93 Burden, 4-52-34—937
47-49 Burdine, 22-75-49—479
56-29 Burgess, 29-39-74—801
10-24 Burke, 30-23-42—242
89-92 Burkes, 8-11-18—667
25-63 Burkley, 32-15-69—393
04-97 Burks, 4-8-11—10C
13-34 Burman, 17-34-47—323
50-75 Burnett, 6-33-64—050
30-75 Burnette, 30-39-53—832
42-56 Burney, 39-58-56—126
78-51 Bumice, 12-7-51—787
91-70 Bums, 21-51-41—170
25-34 Bursey, 6-74-34—647
54-98 Burt, 29-40-54—442
90-92 Burth, 13-67-68—867
13-48 Burton, 13-39-48—448
34-43 Busby, 34-56-72—307
41-42 Bush, 13-41-42—303
28-46 Bushby, 5-10-46—743
47-35 Buster, 17-21-53—352
12-68 Butler, 12-28-59—347
27-33 Butts, 36-72-27—727
79-18 Byrd, 12-18-56—327
05-09 Byrdella, 5-9-55—818
14-21 Byron, 26-35-42—362

# C

38-99 Caballero, 16-38-49—993
36-59 Cabot, 36-50-59—590
89-11 Caddie, 5-11-55—411
58-67 Cade, 48-58-68—364
36-02 Caesar, 2-8-40—284
28-34 Cager, 62-73-76—762
42-88 Cahill, 42-35-45-433
04-50 Cain, 4-10-50—178
03-33 Calderon, 3-11-33—333
46-78 Caldonia, 27-49-78—467
98-29 Caldwell, 29-48-53—853
10-11 Caleb, 10-11-34—134
24-40 Calhoun, 7-11-40—307
15-87 Calixto, 8-18-15—185
66-12 Calle, 37-50-66—053
71-66 Callie, 3-11-71—628
04-57 Calloway, 6-4-39—201
37-59 Caloway, 39-59-47—809
22-77 Calvin, 14-27-59—330

64-97 Calvo, 51-63-64—976
29-69 Camarillo, 28-29-69—622
10-45 Cameron, 19-23-40—040
56-63 Camilla, 38-26-56—365
13 30 Camille, 12-15-30—712
70-74 Camilo, 10-20-30—003
13-86 Cammile, 2-12-13—312
16-13 Camp, 52-61-31—151
54-62 Campbell, 39-54-75—509
35-68 Camper, 39-68-35—638
13-23 Campo, 10-23-13—321
30-43 Canada, 64-67-72—766
29-55 Canadate, 29-74-10—019
67-76 Candace, 1-11-21—111
38-71 Candice, 53-64-71—743
91-14 Candido, 20-30-41—234
65-72 Candie, 40-65-72—650
24-74 Candy, 39-52-68—998
01-61 Canfield, 1-8-19—380
17-31 Cannon, 8-18-27-476
76-36 Cano, 48-59-73—390
54-39 Canty, 30-59-75—395
61-73 Capetta, 39-54-73—370
81-18 Car, 41-66-38—181
15-30 Cardell, 11-21-43—123
07-43 Carelene, 7-19-40—794
32-96 Carey, 49-63-78—347
40-85 Carillo, 54-76-58—745
44-75 Carin, 42-67-75—672
59-13 Carino, 12-43-62—159
26-65 Carl, 71-65-49—781
48-69 Carla, 61-71-69—671
20-80 Carlene, 15-34-20—034
39-44 Carlisle, 50-56-59—592
03-12 Carlita, 3-8-12—283
32-39 Carlo, 9-19-39—210
44-39 Carlos, 44-47-63—281
19-90 Carlota, 4-60-70—400
70-07 Carlotta, 25-30-35—332
52-32 Carlson, 62-21-63—321
60-06 Carlton, 6-27-48—880
11-25 Carlyle, 1-10-36—502
60-34 Carmela, 33-47-60—003
49-81 Carmelita, 14-59-61—184
27-23 Carmella, 3-10-11—135
14-75 Carmen, 23-14-75—357
44-71 Carmillo, 44-53-78—809
14-75 Carmine, 8-46-70—074

11-50 Carol, 24-50-60—524
19-40 Carolina, 6-7-40—480
22-10 Caroline, 16-22-40—401
01-10 Carolyn, 1-10-16—785
43-48 Caron, 45-24-33—431
07-22 Carpenter, 7-18-69—388
40-61 Carpio, 32-58-78—788
33-38 Carr, 47-38-15—105
72-82 Carrasquel, 10-19-71—417
10-21 Carraway, 50-39-53—499
92-95 Carrene, 13-69-72—995
32-96 Carrie, 6-14-32—643
51-65 Carrillo, 28-40-36—905
62-26 Carrol, 23-57-62—257
62-26 Carroll, 13-40-15—004
45-17 Carruth, 7-44-45—574
42-52 Carry, 14-41-71—444
74-10 Carson, 11-10-36—281
20-66 Cartago, 22-39-65—353
41-83 Carter, 6-56-73—760
14-40 Cartmen, 14-40-60—129
08-73 Caruthers, 8-12-40—211
63-93 Carver, 56-46-36—634
37-93 Carvers, 40-53-68—900
75-81 Cary, 31-77-75—775
53-73 Caryl, 68-73-35—373
31-94 Caryn, 22-31-43—294
16-64 Casa, 43-67-12—143
41-84 Casas, 6-16-36—636
25-19 Casaus, 12-55-60—069
32-57 Case, 57-49-63—404
42-60 Casey, 6-46-51—982
39-69 Casilda, 39-69-58—803
74-95 Casper, 1-11-41—309
34-56 Cass, 30-40-50—304
67-72 Cassandra, 17-35-45—504
19-37 Cassidy, 5-19-37—307
09-84 Cassie, 9-19-33—711
96-17 Caster, 14-17-37—731
72-78 Castilla, 33-47-72—006
02-12 Castillo, 3-2-50—302
10-34 Castle, 5-10-36—400
47-69 Castro, 3-13-47—270
28-85 Caswell, 6-10-43—390
10-17 Catalina, 10-17-20—702
58-49 Catharine, 58-62-70—607
58-49 Catherine, 12-4-49—457
48-57 Cathy, 52-63-57—536

68-97 Catlin, 2-5-38—306
18-59 Cato, 34-43-59—819
39-63 Ceasar, 13-73-63—333
12-42 Ceballos, 4-35-12—421
86-68 Cecelia, 62-68-71—682
10-65 Cecil, 10-15-65—659
10-11 Cecile, 8-10-78—632
11-41 Cecelia, 11-19-40—940
70-07 Cecilio, 33-53-70—700
29-92 Cecily, 22-36-59—992
18-98 Cedric, 5-8-44—710
49-57 Ceferino, 61-71-49—411
12-21 Celeste, 12-21-43—980
16-27 Celestine, 7-18-42—842
71-87 Celestino, 7-18-43—878
60-74 Celia, 45-50-60—004
17-78 Celine, 21-60-78—778
19-12 Celso, 12-70-19—120
88-99 Cenderella, 32-44-55—894
40-37 Cenon, 54-67-40—374
88-91 Centeno, 46-68-70—818
15-20 Ceola, 2-15-20—022
15-30 Cerda, 30-59-15^-305
26-37 Cervantes, 20-37-48—732
41-50 Cesar, 69-50-41—504
07-08 Cevil, 3-7-8—378
61-79 Chalmers, 50-51-33—222
66-77 Chambers, 8-11-36—366
35-49 Chandler, 35-49-58—800
16-32 Chaney, 12-16-32—821
26-16 Chanie, 72-52-41—114
06-36 Chaplin, 7-11-66—006
31-72 Chapman, 11-40-59—475
51-89 Chapples, 2-15-69—597
08-16 Charitie, 29-47-56—861
08-16 Charity, 2-8-16—806
41-62 Charleaner, 6-37-55—275
24-46 Charlene, 10-19-24—246
20-25 Charles, 3-20-25—325
50-90 Charleston, 30-50-64—430
33-63 Charleton, 33-54-63—300
16-52 Charley, 16-62-41—849
32-23 Charlie, 7-47-48—232
24-46 Charline, 10-19-24—246
17-67 Charlotte, 4-17-20—207
38-46 Charon, 42-74-46—644
09-39 Chatman, 9-39-47—305
57-92 Chauncey, 15-51-57—927

57-18 Chauncy, 5-23-57—827
27-83 Chavis, 41-64-27—337
16-45 Cheeks, 7-13-45—403
58-12 Cheney, 12-42-39—320
32-42 Cherry, 32-42-69—840
08-77 Chester, 8-18-48—611
31-59 Chick, 4-16-59—223
14-31 Chico, 11-31-48—858
22-37 Chief, 24-75-77—225
73-82 Childres, 37-58-43—300
76-95 Childs, 26-40-56—580
62-74 China, 38-59-74—005
57-18 Chiquita, 10-40-60—817
44-66 Chism, 40-41-70—470
26-33 Chloe, 2-8-16—604
43-75 Choza, 8-37-53—533
81-70 Chris, 13-16-70—700
29-56 Christian, 32-49-55—1T1
15-94 Christina, 12-17-37—370
65-85 Christine, 22-45-49—384
04-06 Christopher, 4-6-10—460
36-72 Chrysler, 23-35-47—490
21-80 Chuck, 3-50-76—218
39-64 Church, 7-11-46—446
39-49 Churchill, 39-49-58—558
55-25 Cianciolo, 58-43-22—555
60-70 Cicely, 1-60-70—700
07-93 Cicero, 7-19-33—818
12-23 Cicily, 3-12-23—223
43-64 Cirilo, 16-25-43—465
24-74 Claiborne, 7-43-54—443
17-35 Claire, 9-39-67—537
95-05 Clancy, 5-10-20—200
13-41 Clara, 13-36-42—420
24-28 Clarabelle, 24-26-28—842
03-63 Clarance, 26-49-39—694
44-54 Clardy, 1-51-54—151
34-62 Clare, 65-77-34—642
3-100 Clarence, 3-5-10—760
18-81 Clarette, 18-27-39—327
24-92 Claribel, 27-57-66—924
29-38 Clarice, 8-11-56—174
29-38 Clarise, 17-78-48—893
25-50 Clarissa, 25-50-53—503
19-63 Clark, 7-10-67—804
41-48 Clarke, 5-48-53—007
53-65 Clarkson, 30-50-73—401
42-73 Clarline, 18-66-73—748

33-91 Classic, 28-56-30—392
08-16 Claude, 8-11-16—769
29-48 Claudette, 31-38-48—435
06-54 Claudio, 6-10-54—369
25-50 Claxton, 25-30-50—303
45-73 Clay, 45-48-59—007
45-48 Clayborne, 31-48-49—603
53-89 Claybourne, 38-75-44—411
03-10 Clayton, 3-10-62—117
62-74 Cleadus, 45-38-60—338
13-26 Clem, 29-52-13—359
37-26 Clement, 10-37-42—142
37-58 Clemente, 38-50-58—150
72-52 Clementine, 5-8-41—912
88-38 Clements, 8-38-58—160
32-37 Clemons, 41-63-37—233
08-80 Cleo, 53-74-80—084
08-61 Cleomedes, 19-61-74—469
18-81 Cleopatra, 7-9-18—981
18-48 Cleophus, 14-48-69—788
44-88 Cleora, 44-54-64—644
04-71 Cleto, 13-30-40—300
16-38 Cleve, 16-38-58—358
99-38 Cleveland, 2-11-27—111
27-51 Gley, 51-62-72—272
19-39 differs, 42-47-49—400
19-79 Clifford, 8-38-49—849
64-54 Clifton, 54-32-29—677
42-83 Climmie, 20-64-42—834
08-98 Clinton, 8-43-27—621
56-87 Clive, 11-18-27—616
06-60 Cloe, 6-11-60—198
70-84 Clorean, 31-42-53—538
20-30 Clorinda, 2-54-75—574
46-54 Clorine, 56-31-43—718
09-50 Clotella, 9-19-50—991
17-77 Clowtee, 1-17-77—187
23-54 Clyde, 4-14-54—616
97-87 Coates, 46-50-70—700
16-38 Cobb, 16-38-57—357
38-58 Cobbs, 9-38-58—983
30-40 Cobina, 30,39-40—493
34-69 Cobos, 43-55-69—435
19-21 Coby, 65-76-55- 555
14-86 Cochran, 14-44-37—864
02-22 Coe, 77-67-41—146
33-47 Coelhos,-31-32-33—347
31-41 Cohan, 31-41-56—305

28-39 Colbert, 39-50-48—301
08-47 Cole, 3-8-47—300
08-48 Coleman, 35-36-48—200
24-40 Coles, 24-40-50—578
47-57 Colesiol, 56-57-47—574
39-56 Colette, 44-66-56—366
10-30 Colie, 28-43-59—349
06-78 Colin, 4-14-74—870
68-74 Colleen, 22-66-68—764
19-96 Collier, 19-22-41—400
15-50 Collins, 2-3-50—332
06-78 Colon, 28-39-78—425
34-36 Colton, 34-36-48—439
25-90 Columbine, 14-19-41—411
14-92 Columbus, 12-18-62—391
14-74 Colvin, 51-41-74—144
05-44 Combes, 18-27-38—472
33-81 Combs, 73-33-12—387
36-54 Commings, 6-50-16—536
63-72 Commodore, 62-72-4—222
24-38 Campbell, 12-24-38—248
19-47 Conan, 49-57-19—457
10-17 Concepcion, 26-17-11—100
43-49 Concha, 37-43-49—943
01-43 Conchita, 1-11-17—010
52-12 Conde, 61-71-43—121
91-96 Condestable, 17-48-5—891
16-46 Connelly, 10-16-46—407
35-55 Connie, 23-37-55—557
10-20 Conrad, 14-20-52—991
36-48 Conrado, 11-36-48—843
25-55 Constance, 25-55-76—550
31-82 Constancia, 60-70-75—576
25-23 Constant, 33-25-23—233
16-92 Constantia, 5-25-16—915
16-13 Constantine, 3-13-55—335
11-75 Consuela, 47-49-51—547
64-54 Consuelo, 28-32-54—832
05-57 Conway, 5-10-57—557
11-22 Cook, 31-11-22—222
9-100 Cooke, 24-69-70—070
54-83 Coolidge, 14-40-36—787
17-37 Cooper, 25-37-59—357
76-93 Copley, 16-59-76—671
49-57 Coppin, 39-49-73—404
56-65 Cora, 1-56-39—599
30-41 Coral, 35-46-53—434
12-69 Coralee, 60-69-70—760

12-42 Coramae, 7-12-15—257
30-42 Corbin, 3-42-45—433
42-54 Cordelia, 42-54-63—634
30-59 Corbett, 52-38-59—300
84-91 Cordell, 68-70-17—918
94-66 Cordie, 10-58-66—669
03-48 Cordoba, 3-13-11—480
35-48 Cordova, 45-48-53—358
77-22 Corean, 78-77:67—276
10-29 Coreen, 23-34-29—923
10-56 Corene, 34-56-60—012
69-59 Corine, 9-69-59—646
59-85 Corinna, 53-59-58—555
15-40 Corinne, 57-62-40—415
95-05 Corinthia, 5-41-42—463
14-67 Corley, 15-67-14—674
07-37 Corliss, 29-37-51—542
19-29 Cornelia, 8-19-29—173
60-72 Cornelius, 13-60-72—613
11-37 Cornell, 35-11-46—600
78-84 Corredor, 70-78-68—778
25-30 Corrie, 14-25-27—230
100-2 Corrine, 10-20-30—000
11-52 Cortes, 66-43-52—416
16-26 Cortez, 5-35-57—625
36-92 Cortina, 42-36-29-423
43-79 Corwin, 35-49-58—409
14-44 Cosetta, 14-40-44—482
24-76 Cosgrove, 17-24-34—342
06-16 Cossie, 24-32-54—160
43-57 Costa, 15-41-57—415
57-73 Costello, 23-34-56—503
15-20 Coswell, 63-72-51—726
43-93 Cotas, 31-43-64—493
33-46 Cotton, 3-23-40—323
11-12 Counce, 11-12-46—217
16-61 Councella, 16-32-49—621
70-82 Count, 8-10-6—879
80-56 Counts, 10-18-56—560
12-56 Courtney, 9-11-56—671
19-59 Cousey, 11-19-59—119
38-41 Cowan, 35-49-50—400
32-40 Cowans, 64-51-40—056
03-53 Cowherd, 6-39-53—396
23-45 Cox, 22-30-45—223
18-81 Cozetta, 17-16-18—678
29-31 Cozette, 29-31-50—-43
14-21 Craft, 42-16-7—380

35-40 Crafton, 40-35-58—488
10-12 Craig, 1-2-12—011
14-62 Craighead, 13-17-20—379
22-44 Crane, 15-22-44—407
94-82 Cravis, 18-13-29—212
70-71 Crawford, 56-71-34—812
21-38 Crayton, 21-15-38—107
31-62 Creola, 30-49-65—305
43-57 Cris, 13-40-57—350
20-46 Crisis, 19-40-46—C07
39-63 Crisostomo, 46-74-78—509
06-16 Crisp, 6-16-19—140
54-95 Crissie, 38-46-54—386
13-72 Cristina, 2-29-72—223
08-18 Cristobal, 12-21-47—808
40-53 Cristoval, 14-40-67—560
23-32 Crockett, 9-19-23—414
47-56 Croford, 3-5-9—003
22-36 Crooke, 22-24-36—8C1
12-64 Crosley, 3-10-30—300
14-84 Cross, 2-14-17-400
41-55 Crowder, 29-40-59—403
35-39 Cruise, 33-35-39—390
30-96 Crum, 1-15-28—132
39-26 Crumb, 13-26-38—352
35-59 Crump, 18-27-50—372
26-91 Cruthcr, 33-46-26—912
07-77 Cruthers, 4-9-77—777
17-51 Cruz, 25-51-63—651
55-69 Crystain, 15-43-52—554
35-51 Crystal, 35-43-51—541
42-56 Cullins, 34-56-76—-08
34-76 Cumire, 73-76-46—764
90-64 Cunningham, 7-16-6—311
58-82 Curley, 13-24-58—349
37-58 Curlie, 14-39-58—830
68-91 Curnvester, 10-16-49—324
10-30 Curry, 11-30-46—455
76-47 Curtis, 25-34-45—669
05-50 Custodio, 5-50-51—551
59-89 Cutler, 12-20-43—230
43-62 Cybelle, 16-20-29—926
12-67 Cynthia, 8-56-49—652
18-58 Cypriano, 44-58-31—581
10-50 Cyril, 18-34-50—543
49-75 Cyrilla, 5-6-7—605
27-83 Cyrus, 74-61-50—746

# D

41-69 Dabbs, 31-7-69—789
59-89 Dabney, 49-59-62—441
07-11 Dade, 7-11-20—806
44-88 Dagmar, 8-26-38—826
47-57 Dailey, 37-47-57—695
99-23 Daisy, 9-53-41—818
42-66 Dalaney, 5-43-50—717
19-74 Dale, 3-27-52—508
44-55 Dallas, 5-11-55—779
15-50 Dalton, 15-50-78—317
87-63 Damaso, 67-70-30—006
30-40 Damian, 22-40-30—402
40-69 Damon, 19-47-55—765
73-98 Dan, 27-66-73—798
18-69 Dancey, 17-35-69—410
15-88 Danella, 12-14-44—414
33-69 Daniel, 51-63-69—569
69-35 Daniels, 14-31-35—771
28-86 Dangerfield, 28-33-4—382
18-36 Dannie, 19-35-36—539
18-36 Danny, 72-60-41—147
14-48 Dantley, 1-7-14—841
12-20 Daphne, 10-12-20—221
54-72 Darby, 39-45^72—819
43-56 Darden, 13-43-54—593
18-36 Dardenella, 36-46-52—638
48-57 Darlene, 11-48-57—400
44-51 Darling, 10-18-44—104
79-97 Darnell, 43-56-48—507
66-77 Darnella, 32-14-77—28'
21-85 Darryl, 20-45-63—456
06-26 Darwin, 44-68-24—394
04-65 Dastalfo, 13-23-43—323
29-43 Dasy, 28-37-49—792
38-41 Daugherty, 38-41-42—422
94-97 Daughtry, 59-69-77—9'7
21-29 Daukins, 70-29-39—212
26-83 Dave, 34-44-62—836
50-66 Davenport, 27-57-52—513
09-19 Davett, 9-19-37—098
43-93 Davia, 22-43-57—543
41-57 David, 7-8-72—782
44-33 Davidson, 11-44-33—311
9-100 Davie, 45-56-57—179
14-70 Davies, 45-56-57—179
28-34 Davila, 14-47-58—147

16-78 Davis, 8-10-78—189
71-82 Davison, 39-48-53—402
08-18 Dawes, 8-18-37—337
14-58 Dawkins, 51-78-14—715
37-84 Dawn, 3-21-37—387
57-62 Dawson, 8-17-52—412
10-15 Day, 10-15-49—709
23-34 Daza, 48-58-34—324
37-82 D'Costa, 30-37-51—287
02-14 Dean, 14-36-47—443
10-72 Deatter, 8-35-72—001
35-66 Debid, 66-77-44—665
29-70 Deborah, 29-47-55—440
43-57 Debra, 20-29-57—573
15-51 Debruce, 12-50-51—150
27-37 Deede, 27-37-42—437
41-51 Deese, 27-37-51—277
30-59 Degrate, 30-59-63—359
56-70 Delaney, 10-11-70—299
25-75 Delano, 25-75-78—878
34-90 Delcie, 8-11-46—932
26-85 Delfina, 36-65-78—856
18-38 Delia, 8-18-38—681
43-73 Delicia, 49-56-43—549
43-12 Delifus, 19-28-39—829
13-33 Delilah, 9-18-33—691
10-20 Della, 2-10-32—614
52-86 Delmar, 43-52-86—523
06-86 Delmira, 43-52-6—860
60-68 Delmonaco, 60-68-70—060
44-39 Deloach, 18-37-50—504
15-74 Delone, 64-71-74—715
15-50 DeLong, 15-50-8—500
96-82 Delores, 20-30-43—342
14-19 Deloris, 8-19-53—824
87-78 Delphia, 3-13-36—572
36-20 Delphine, 9-33-52—253
10-20 Delplina, 10-20-40—414
25-37 Delta, 76-67-57—676
16-43 Demecio, 27-38-72—167
44-88 Demetrius, 11-17-44—888
05-75 Democracia, 4-14-75—051
57-75 Demostenes, 73-57-2—575
41-51 Dempsey, 27-40-51—599
65-49 Dendy, 60-53-42—605
07-69 Denese, 38-18-12—281
42-69 Denesee, 38-42-53—543
32-56 Denigan, 69-71-68—668

40-70 Denis, 33-40-70—347
22-70 Denise, 33-40-70—007
82-95 Denmon, 7-46-28—829
68-11 Dennis, 4-11-57—774
68-71 Dennison, 43-54-58—580
03-92 Denny, 32-61-29—032
69-99 Dent, 8-45-69—876,
55-38 Dentham, 13-68-74—763
13-27 Deona, 62-66-72—137
40-64 Depriest, 23-77-64—604
33-81 Desdemona, 15-45-59—333
08-18 Desdemonia, 8-11-18—631
27-54 Desiree, 2-31-54—724
20-35 Desla, 20-24-35—-025
98-67 Desmond, 6-44-67—698
80-48 Dessimer, 52-48-44—912
63-71 Develmor, 9-29-41—509
45-54 Devine, 32-54-65—400
39-91 Dewey, 31-29-40—163
10-12 DeWitt, 76-61-10—100
20-54 Dexter, 4-11-40—409
19-32 Diamond, 43-32-19—913
13-20 Diana, 8-13-20—813
13-79 Diane, 63-70-61—766
47-56 Dias, 24-47-56—-75
01-47 Diaz, 42-53-47-475
23-10 Dick, 1-75-53—102
10-62 Dickens, 4-10-50—455
10-54 Dickerson, 13-32-54—311
32-54 Dickinson, 3-32-54—311
32-46 Dickson, 13-44-55—144
11-38 Dicy, 16-11-38—831
18-78 Diego, 5-25-41—788
29-49 Dill, 29-37-49—468
97-80 Dillard, 1-6-10—328
15-97 Dilliard, 15-9-29—312
60-90 Dimes, 44-50-72—333
31-43 Dimple, 4-19-41—509
05-55 Dinah, 5-9-55—714
57-77 Dink, 8-18-42—678
04-14 Dionisio, 40-50-44—444
53-69 Distasio, 10-14-54—433
45-61 Dixie, 8-45-51—190
45-17 Dixon, 4-11-17—802
35-89 Dobankia, 35-72-39—408
24-37 Docila, 14-40-59—402
17-37 Docilla, 55-74-37—317
76-82 Doctor, 26-39-76—269

03-13 Dodd, 3-31-53—423
33-48 Dodge, 12-32-48—818
36-48 Dogan, 36-45-48—444
36-59 Doheny, 26-36-49—431
32-17 Dolarite, 19-26-41—962
13-33 Doll, 13-33-47—433
08-13 Dollie, 8-13-63—721
14-79 Dollor, 12-35-14—145
08-13 Dolly, 8-13-63—721
52-15 Dolores, 15-25-52—555
25-52 Dolorosa, 15-25-52—552
58-49 Dolton, 4-12-49—800
18-48 Dominga, 18-48-49—948
23-31 Domingo, 40-42-46—446
16-42 Dominguez, 7-11-42—241
34-43 Dominic, 34-43-48—443
34-43 Dominick, 34-43-52—334
14-34 Dominico, 43-34-14—414
44-14 Dominicus, 14-44-54—514
53-69 Dominus, 30-53-69—334
02-30 Don, 5-11-55—799
34-88 Dona, 5-11-46—145
48-80 Donah, 3-20-36—002
15-99 Donald, 27-53-72—191
40-50 Donalds, 12-40-50—405
40-78 Donaldson, 12-35-78—498
22-81 Doniel, 27-39-61—619
14-93 Donna, 14-70-63—473
10-70 Donnell, 10-6-70 590
10-29 Donnelly, 11-32-57—450
70-80 Donnie, 14-70-74—774
16-47 Donohue, 36-57-69—965
94-89 Dooley, 12-43-56—468
45-64 Doolittle, 23-45-64—300
41-81 Dora, 6-40-60—00
57-98 Doraine, 15-21-31—115
63-40 Dorcas, 28-41-71—280
13-71 Dorch, 2-6-13—311
90-95 Dorchester, 15-44-57—411
46-52 Doresey, 46-61-52—526
61-73 Doressa, 73-61-46—461
13-95 Doreste, 24-48-67—709
44-56 Dorethea, 16-38-52—258
19-84 Doriene, 38-44-66—663
12-18 Dorinda, 12-18-42—617
28-65 Doris, 4-10-65—217
39-21 Doroteo, 39-60-12—069
60-80 Dorothea, 39-50-21—080

60-66 Dorothy, 11-12-16—111
62-91 Dorris, 4-10-65—217
45-72 D'Orsay, 7-12-20—452
49-55 Dorsey, 49-52-55—622
64-79 Dorthy, 11-64-16—111
50-55 Dossie, 5-50-55—523
71-82 Doswell, 22-32-37—328
12-16 Dot, 3-53-27—551
92-60 Dotsie, 46-56-72—387
63-73 Dotson, 7-15-32—811
11-34 Doty, 1-11-16—910
42-68 Dougherty, 38-5-46—422
33-66 Douglas, 45-62-39—545
40-58 Dove, 26-40-58—566
40-58 Dovie, 7-11-15—512
15-55 Dow, 55-66-67—951
24-42 Downer, 10-40-50—500
50-78 Doyle, 8-12-50—615
67-15 Dozier, 53-58-70—480
27-57 Drake, 27-5-42—312
48-16 Drayfis, 11-48-29—114
29-48 Drayfris, 11-48-58—801
87-34 Drayfus, 11-29-34—291
49-72 Drayton, 30-49-72—480
10-77 Drew, 18-39-56—422
43-72 Drews, 22-40-72—272
59-34 Driscoll, 38-59-62—583
68-86 Driver, 8-37-59—802
66-71 Drucilla, 7-11-79—946
25-51 Drummer, 36-29-51—153
16-36 Drummond, 31-36-6—488
23-56 Drusilla, 4-8-23—536
35-90 Dryden, 13-45-64—803
76-43 Duarte, 9-18-25—819
06-66 Duboise, 6-11-66—842
18-52 Duckett, 25-40-69—008
85-65 Duckworth, 11-44-65—556
37-67 Duddley, 37-57-67—320
14-41 Dudley, 14-41-71—176
01-95 Duff, 1-11-49—941
01-49 Duffle, 11-40-49—433
69-12 Duke, 35-56-69—490
12-17 Dukes, 12-4-8—709
26-30 Dulce, 27-30-67—990
30-65 Dulcie, 6-14-56—891
11-36 Dumas, 10-11-33—384
36-45 Duncan, 12-36-45—210
53-29 Dunlap, 9-19-29—369

32-84 Dunn, 16-32-55—677
36-46 Dunnaway, 26-36-46—466
19-75 Dunson, 24-34-43—243
44-16 Dupree, 15-16-22—226
97-54 Duquesa, 38-45-50—500
11-94 Durando, 10-17-28—017
58-61 Durham, 35-58-74—604
27-64 Durkins, 7-13-27—^427
18-63 Durr, 49-54-63—674
37-83 Dus, 16-44-68—481
50-59 Dutton, 39-50-59—359
27-45 Duvall, 5-13-27—518
08-18 Dwight, 8-18-78—987
55-20 Dwise, 33-66-76-637
93-74 Dyanne, 1-8-74—174
45-96 Dyck, 23-43-45—442
38-48 Dyer, 17-37-48—891

# E

15-52 Earl, 6-15-52—123
15-46 Earleen, 29-46-50—287
15-67 Earlie, 42-51-61—112
15-46 Earline, 23-34-46—436
99-43 Early, 17-20-43—-24
28-91 Earnestine, 22-3-7—821
25-48 Easter, 25-40-48—322
25-40 Eastman, 25-40-60—430
10-36 Eatman, 45-55-65—880
11-12 Eaton, 11-43-46—300
98-47 Eaves, 45-69-52—640
03-84 Eben, 13-32-48—438
20-82 Ebenezer, 8-23-27—101
40-50 Eclair, 12-40-50—304
77-56 Ector, 21-31-52—756
19-37 Eddie, 18-49-52—787
13-67 Eddy, 35-67-39—711
16-74 Edelmira, 71-74-64—644
08-97 Edelmiro, 8-43-51—040
48-62 Eden, 5-17-45—780
29-35 Edgar, 8-35-74—874
69-96 Edie, 44-37-21—127
83-28 Edieth, 22-28-63—306
83-28 Edith, 22-28-63—306
11-90 Edmonds, 62-63-69—966
11-13 Edmund, 6-11-13—613
38-67 Edmundo, 30-53-67—537
17-27 Edna, 27-32-40—483
17-57 Ednamae, 17-87-54—817

27-96 Edrea, 44-72-27—247
35-48 Edward, 35-48-74-874
35-48 Edward, 35-48-74—874
57-17 Edwards, 11-15-41—114
19-21 Edwin, 30-56-61—361
42-89 Edwina, 7-37-67—535
15-75 Effie, 29-48-63—550
22-39 Egas, 22-45-55—888
01-49 Egbert, 72-43-13—337
58-79 Eileen, 58-5-55—585
18-42 Elaine, 35-54-63—183
30-60 Elam, 53-57-67—418
18-68 Elane, 18-28-68—288
18-42 Elaync, 1-55-42—251
31-95 Elbert, 31-53-65—570
31-76 Elberta, 64-76-67—667
74-93 Elcano, 15-20-25—502
40-50 Elden, 4-11-50—876
52-59 Elder, 52-59-61—995
23-37 Elders, 3-23-37—337
39-48 Eldora, 36-73-75—333
14-56 Eldorado, 14-56-64—624
69-77 Eldons, 28-65-56—977
60-51 Eleanor, 4-49-63—113
23-88 Eleazar, 23-45-48—238
37-56 Electa, 7-37-56—812
06-41 Elena, 6-29-66—416
04-14 Elens, 24-33-44—404
21-85 Elex, 21-4-27—724
92-17 Elfrieda, 46-49-72—790
77-83 Elgetha, 51-32-12—122
41-33 Eli, 3-60-70—669
27-49 Eliabeth, 50-60-71—000
45-55 Elias, 45-55-69—904
61-73 Eligah, 20-41-61—164
13-46 Elihu, 13-33-46—334
35-57 Elijah, 15-24-51—521
07-10 Elinor, 1-7-10—101
05-81 Elisa, 40-60-78—078
05-26 Elise, 5-53-32—822
45-55 Elisha, 18-22-68—826
17-67 Elissa, 49-70-67—716
54-78 Elissia, 33-47-64—448
02-23 Elita, 12-39-59—232
18-49 Elitra, 2-18-49—432
70-72 Eliza, 2-25-70—207
88-96 Elizabeth, 5-8-61—601
80-87 Ella, 6-9-14—912

34-43 Ellamae, 77-43-34—347
18-56 Ellen, 9-56-13—615
44-50 Eller, 69-70-50—219
25-93 Ellett, 2-18-25—218
06-11 Elliot, 6-11-56—605
06-12 Elliott, 12-20-40—801
33-53 Ellis, 45-62-53—673
54-58 Ellissie, 3-19-54—193
46-71 Ellsworth, 18-33-49—849
49-50 Elma, 49-50-69—798
53-78 Elmer, 1-14-66—146
22-62 Elmeto, 38-48-62—147
06-10 Elmo, 9-8-10—260
24-52 Elmore, 25-30-42—781
86-43 Elna, 76-30-12—417
18-32 Elnora, 32-53-61—496
47-05 Eloi, 58-68-8—500
94-79 Eloine, 17-37-16—949
21-67 Eloise, 21-67-45—595
57-83 Eloy, 14-31-47—413
14-31 Elphina, 3-10-31—330
14-19 Elpidio, 75-66-23—267
66-32 Elrenia, 6-13-66—801
52-68 Elrich, 14-68-52—808
70-24 Elroy, 70-26-33—033
08-12 Elsa, 8-12-24—191
42-61 Elselina, 57-67-70—765
08-12 Elsie, 12-15-31—261
25-52 Elston, 7-16-18—167
13-33 Elva, 3-13-33—333
42-57 Elverta, 57-27-74—774
09-87 Elvira, 14-19-20—919
20-63 Ely, 2-10-20—200
17-78 Elzir, 46-51-62—254
26-67 Emagine, 78-67-43—787
04-10 Emanuel, 5-10-25—532
62-57 Emanuela, 21-41-51—511
06-66 Embry, 4-31-56—604
24-74 Emeline, 11-16-74—436
33-90 Emely, 29-63-33—369
11-36 Emerson, 2-11-50—812
27-96 Emery, 30-60-62—541
18-27 Emil, 53-62-72—627
18-27 Emile, 38-45-62—458
74-66 Emilia, 5-13-66—746
12-30 Emiliano, 17-72-47—274
56-82 Emilio, 28-39-56—936
18-27 Emily, 5-41-56—405

14-44 Emma, 51-54-74—407
15-50 Emmanuel, 15-45-50—551
16-25 Emmert, . 18-39-52—259
35-89 Emmet, 61-66-70—617
33-42 Emmett, 7-10-42—668
20-59 Emmylou, 24-52-41—145
72-95 Emogene, 9-56-42—086
65-78 Emory, 46-65-78—447
49-81 Encarnacion, 3-6-9—693
02-65 England, 5-10-56—718
55-73 Engracia, 14-55-63—456
13-23 Engram, 13-32-40—843
43-88 Enid, 3-5-7—742
67-41 Enise, 40-50-67—050
47-62 Ennis, 10-47-62—410
12-14 Enos, 73-53-33—537
67-74 Enrica, 14-44-57—415
67-84 Enrico, 64-43-69—844
13-25 Enriel, 3-13-43—642
34-44 Enrique, 23-34-44—324
24-34 Enriqueta, 7-14-21—147
20-80 Eola, 58-62-53—628
15-30 Ephraim, 13-15-39—550
15-30 Ephriam, 1-30-73—173
72-86 Epitacia, 41-72-74—772
35-64 Eppie, 11-33-58—459
10-19 Epps, 10-19-45—810
14-94 Era, 31-74-39—471
7-100 Erasmus, 48-52-76—476
17-27 Erastus, 7-10-57—852
48-87 Eric, 21-31-46—121
09-82 Erica, 51-65-68—651
41-51 Erler, 2-42-57-422
15-54 Erlinger, 5-8-10—390
63-79 Erma, 10-15-52—217
06-16 Ernes, 10-16-6—804
38-45 Ernest, 38-45-55—855
38-49 Ernestine, 10-27-49—37C
33-56 Ernesto, 6-15-56—842
23-71 Errol, 8-16-32—268
05-42 Ersaline, 4-5-45—180
76-83 Erskine, 5-19-45—901
40-46 Erva, 71-60-54—706
56-62 Ervin, 6-54-39—935
56-49 Erwin, 37-43-61—433
21-75 Escobar, 27-46-73—721
31-37 Escribano, 3-11-33—313
10-60 Eshleen, 10-14-60—876

16-45 Esmeralda, 12-24-36—426
33-83 Espana, 19-39-47—991
03-52 Espeja, 59-70-77—070
47-58 Esperanza, 4-14-56—416
17-97 Espinola, 26-37-42—736
18-68 Espinoza, 30-36-53—330
12-21 Espiovel, 4-59-71—179
40-51 Esquire, 44-60-40—440
91-82 Esren, 47-59-63—954
30-40 Essex, 39-34-56—110
07-77 Essie, 7-14-48—623
56-38 Essiena, 1-10-60—723
22-39 Estanislao, 8-18-20—818
29-56 Esteban, 25-35-45—324
56-67 Estebanez, 16-32-41—361
21-59 Estee, 55-68-39—856
01-17 Estella, 6-11-49—534
57-84 Estelle, 32-44-48—443
32-36 Ester, 32-34-36—432
10-36 Estes, 43-16-10—361
60-39 Estevao, 48-39-60—096
52-78 Esteves, 76-43-10—100
36-66 Esther, 36-62-66—606
83-98 Estrada, 1-4-7—774
19-28 Ethan, 20-34-43—203
96-69 Ethel, 5-9-49—543
18-92 Ethell, 67-69-59—997
43-57 Ethelbert, 10-15-38—501
16-85 Ethelee, 16-60-65—582
17-61 Ethelyn, 42-53-60—342
11-53 Etta, 9-11-53—765
33-46 Ettinger, 10-33-62—599
40-60 Eubanks, 5-9-60—309
08-77 Euclid, 21-56-77—627
15-55 Eudora, 16-36-55—110
22-70 Eufarla, 12-17-60—371
13-14 Eufaula, 4-14-42—483
62-47 Eufracio, 43-49-47—934
34-68 Eugene, 34-68-69—369
36-56 Eugenia, 36-56-78—654
36-56 Eugenie, 50-75-56—755
36-56 Eugenio, 3-22-36—223
37-86 Eugune, 66-73-68—668
56-41 Eula, 9-20-31-=-818
62-78 Eulalia, 7-75-78-412
04-63 Eular, 39-52-64—364
27-93 Eulm, 14-39-72—934
33-99 Eulogia, 9-32-33—993

96-83 Eunice, 1-18-51—111
05-15 Euplemia, 5-15-55—354
24-82 Eura, 34-67-72—276
09-73 Eusebio, 8-45-73—458
27-37 Eustace, 27-37-50—235
37-50 Eustacia, 27-37-50—235
37-50 Eustacio, 27-37-50—235
29-62 Eutopia, 24-56-62—246
05-15 Eva, 61-56-49—924
72-23 Evan, 8-14-33—148
40-43 Evans, 13-22-43—408
60-70 Evangeline, 9-60-70—900
51-81 Evar, 1-13-54—511
42-39 Evaristo, 68-78-42—886
56-65 Eve, 18-56-65—650
18-36 Evelina, 46-65-68—646
21-80 Evelino, 3-21-33—221
17-77 Evelyn, 27-48-77—767
38-89 Everardo, 7-69-70—697
07-11 Everett, 7-11-59—790
19-49 Everlena, 9-19-49—868
36-63 Evers, 12-21-52—441
16-52 Evie, 31-52-16—153
04-06 Excelentísima, 2-4-6—462
04-08 Excelentísimo, 2-4-8—842
79-97 Ezekiel, 11-33-67—137
06-25 Ezell, 69-66-6—696
16-48 Ezequiel, 47-16-66—174
90-64 Ezra, 57-64-14—756

# F

17-70 Faber, 17-70-71—707
28-37 Fabian, 70-77-37—077
47-74 Fabienne, 9-18-36—819
02-57 Fair, 12-42-57—421
83-65 Fairfax, 16-65-66—566
78-52 Faith, 8-11-52—522
79-62 Falco, 34-48-57—487
79-82 Falcoes, 42-77-70—077
11-22 Falls, 2-11-22—232
98-26 Falquez, 51-60-70—605
44-45 Fannie, 13-45-56—455
44-50 Fanny, 1844-50—180
39-53 Farfan, 48-53-39—538
17-36 Faria, 17-71-36—171
12-75 Farias, 4-12-16—216
07-66 Farina, 28-58-66—580
27-91 Farlow, 10-20-31—791

12-20 Farmer, 8-12-20—755
04-84 Faulk, 72-44-4-474
04-11 Faulkner, 4-11-55—333
14-41 Faust, 14-41-73—413
19-46 Faustine, 59-73-66—739
19-54 Faustino, 18-29-39—298
29-47 Fay, 29-38-47—610
29-76 Faye, 6-50-63—506
41-99 Feaster, 1-2-8—128
20-50 Fedelia, 12-20-50—519
95-61 Federico, 4-10-55—184
30-41 Federigo, 55-66-72—567
04-14 Felice, 3-4-7—443
60-50 Felicia, 65-7-43—756
38-49 Feliciana, 7-16-37—168
19-38 Feliciano, 7-16-37—981
22-71 Felipe, 23-35-22—232
02-05 Felise, 32-54-50—030
05-66 Felix, 2-5-66—256
45-56 Felton, 45-56-68-420
49-17 Ferd, 12-17-50—870
59-71 Ferdie, 44-56-71—923
17-24 Ferdinand, 2-6-24—264
37-42 Fergus, 37-42-73—347
33-42 Ferguson, 33-45-57—711
16-81 Fermin, 28-32-66—866
18-61 Fem, 10-18-61—712
18-31 Feman, 36-44-31—431
11-14 Fernandes, 13-33-14—133
11-14 Fernandez, 2-13-14—413
42-70 Fernando, 13-242—314
10-79 Ferran, 53-64-67—647
49-65 Ferris, 15-49-65—459
53-88 Ferry, 15-42-53—469
17-35 Ferryman, 17-18-35—784
58-32 Ferguson, 22-32-58—232
20-94 Fester, 25-37-48—473
01-69 Feyra, 1-52-63—521
57-87 Fidel, 43-76-63—363
13-43 Fidelia, 12-13-43—431
05-08 Field, 5-8-40—540
33-40 Fielding, 5-8-40—540
05-08 Fields, 39-59-69—339
44-55 Fifi, 44-55-77—477
32-57 Figueroa, 21-32-57—327
78-83 Filippa, 75-76-78—766
68-69 Fillmore, 11-40-69—169
86-44 Filomena, 38-41-44—413

01-99 Finley, 26-62-73—260
1-100 Finney, 2-10-22—616
35-50 Firestone, 25-35-50—308
68-84 Fisher, 39-49-68—199
34-93 Fitch, 20-27-10—727
44-58 Fitz, 17-44-58—459
56-65 Fitzgerald, 2-44-45—697
54-08 Fitzjames, 15-30-54—431
31-62 Fitzpatrick, 31-69-72—272
85-77 Fitzroy, 42-77-16—724
27-46 Fitzsimmons, 8-27-46—592
18-67 Flamenco, 40-49-67—694
03-35 Flavia, 5-19-37—483
35-54 Fleetwood, 35-46-54—492
63-92 Fleming, 11-74-63—371
63-78 Flemings, 60-63-70—366
55-75 Fleshman, 30-40-55—545
46-56 Fletcher, 32-45-56—553
09-72 Flo, 54-72-63—092
82-56 Floella, 41-56-62—546
15-43 Floorie, 15-17-43—352
42-03 Flora, 8-12-45—487
37-46 Florabel, 62-46-30—304
37-46 Florabelle, 6-71-46—676
73-90 Florance, 30-40-57—439
57-24 Fiorella, 53-77-24—735
07-17 Florence, 7-17-56—653
27-33 Florencio, 70-33-27—377
51-84 Florene, 42-48-51—481
56-49 Florenz, 14-56-49—563
56-93 Florenza, 12-13-10—410
43-58 Florette, 33-43-58—834
91-74 Florez, 63-47-23—769
25-50 Floria, 14-12-6—502
10-16 Florian, 29-69-70—079
17-71 Florida, 35-46-71—841
57-17 Florine, 17-57 49—812
59-64 Florit, 78-64-39—548
34-83 Flossie, 3-11-53—614
6-100 Flournoy, 43-64-23—436
96-83 Flower, 4-28-38—884
52-83 Flowers, 66-9-7—963
17-75 Floy, 8-17-72—817
07-17 Floyd, 7-17-57—142
26-60 Flozell, 15-34-43—435
17-44 Fonda, 44-55-10—541
52-69 Forbes, 12-52-69—440
40-55 Ford, 31-40-55—602

04-35 Foreman, 32-54-65—432
12-41 Forest, 12-8-41—401
11-12 Forrest, 11-19-50—405
15-69 Fort, 14-15-69—819
15-45 Forte, 45-57-68—374
07-17 Fortune, 7-17-57—123
11-61 Foster, 8-48-68—780
27-36 Fountain, 11-45-60—867
74-77 Foushie, 8-74-77—774
62-92 Fowler, 15-32-67—109
18-84 Fox, 13-41-9—804
45-33 Frances, 6-17-33—633
05-37 Francetta, 48-63-71—486
27-34 Francine, 9-27-34—482
11-18 Francis, 11-16-18—168
10-11 Francisca, 7-10-17—710
11-17 Francisco, 11-17-23—372
35-76 Franco, 7-16-45—617
35-63 Francos, 35-43-9—460
35-45 Francois, 24-35-45—354
28-55 Frania, 5-55-72—823
42-59 Frank, 42-38-59—909
42-50 Frankenstein, 5-8-3—500
14-41 Frankie, 14-41-54—310
100-8 Franklin, 2-10-37—862
43-89 Fray, 31-40-43—403
40-57 Frazier, 9-40-57—454
95-55 Frazzie, 11-44-29—108
02-71 Fread, 20-39-2—200
08-28 Fred, 52-61-28-826
08-28 Freda, 8-28-42—842
14-41 Freddie, 21-59-63—211
88-23 Frederic, 31-56-75—365
08-54 Frederica, 5-9-60—006
70-81 Frederick, 38-51-76—715
17-57 Fredonia, 7-17-57—964
32-49 Fredrica, 6-8-10—659
11-22 Freeman, 2-11-22—651
04-08 Freland, 2-4-8—110
40-69 Fremont, 19-27-17—912
46-56 French, 34-46-56—566
33-46 Frenchia, 10-18-33—433
33-42 Frenchie, 66-42-19—453
22-99 Frey, 50-59-20—559
01-94 Friday, 3-8-75—837
48-80 Frieda, 26-37-30—307
98-68 Frisby, 38-59-68—488
38-68 Fritz, 18-72-38—575

13-63 Fraila, 49-58-13—588
31-53 Froilaz, 18-25-20—258
13-32 Frost, 13-32-45—345
78-87 Fructuoso, 58-74-78—877
67-29 Fruto, 19-29-6-400
39-79 Fuentes, 36-48-39—483
54-87 Fulford, 28-32-54—280
86-21 Fulgencio, 2-24-21—121
19-38 Fuller, 19-38-25—109
07-66 Fulton, 8-31-42—322
93-57 Furgerson, 6-19-57—460

# G

74-47 Gabbie, 36-41-62—667
43-49 Gables, 5-12-49-412
30-65 Gabriel, 6-15-78—856
38-49 Gabriela, 38-49-56—101
40-49 Gabriella, 14-40-71—500
38-53 Gabrielle, 23-38-53—538
20-78 Gadsden, 65-42-13—134
12-24 Gadson, 14-17-60—600
02-22 Gahr, 21-5740—075
67-73 Gail, 35-47-56-473
38-68 Gaillard, 1-73-56—476
85-58 Gaines, 4-23-58—407
67-73 Gale, 68-67-73—377
38-46 Galindo, 17-38-46—486
19-69 Gallegher, 56-16-22—162
06-97 Galloway, 46-67-6—674
77-87 Galo, 22-77-61—172
29-64 Gamble, 10-69-59—383
48-67 Gandara, 3748-67—367
66-70 Gandy, 9-56-70—796
29-87 Gant, 15-41-69—341
17-67 Garay, 52-37-67—763
47-58 Garci, 43-73-47—374
83-78 Garcia, 11-33-78—313
62-83 Garcias, 64-56-72—628
28-96 Garcilaso, 22-53-38—532
43-55 Garcilasso, 2-4-55—505
48-59 Gardner, 10-48-59—435
21-76 Garfield, 2-1645—701
39-50 Gamer, 21-39-50—268
55-66 Garnett, 14-56-72-472
09-19 Garret, 9-19-36—801
14-55 Garrett, 14-45-61—390
38-18 Garrison, 38-18-28—181
18-38 Garrity, 7-18-38—830

04-75 Gartley, 43-27-75—243
10-88 Gartrell, 12-30-41—303
50-60 Gary, 19-60-59—912
36-65 Gaspar, 65-52-37—525
39-93 Gaston, 2-54-39—249
44-50 Gately, 1644-50—432
15-63 Gates, 3-8-20—818
05-15 Gateward, 34-44-15—144
19-54 Gawson, 12-33-54—333
63-74 Gay. 74-63-36—667
52-69 Gayle, 13-54-69—988
42-43 Gaylord, 4243-56—501
78-89 Gayoso, 18-26-32—820
11-78 Gazola, 8-11-78—798
33-66 Gean, 9-69-59—005
20-31 Gebaldi, 20-27-31—720
03-57 Geboney, 45-55-66—546
63-97 Gee, 75-62-63—797
53-81 Gene, 35-53-18—813
11-64 Genesee, 14-24-33—241
32-73 Geneva, 6-34-27—816
24-56 Genevieve, 6-56-39—719
27-72 Genora, 18-38-26—836
18-90 Geoffrey, 24-76-64—764
18-38 Geoffry, 2-18-38—238
21-79 George, 24-6—246
04-40 Georgette, 10-21-32—909
63-14 Georgia, 34-14-22—691
56-69 Georgiana, 12-28-75—125
72-98 Georgiann, 46-56-62—256
12-52 Georgianna, 6-25-52—552
33-91 Georgina, 36-77-33—373
80-62 Gerald, 67-71-62—C01
07-14 Geraldine, 7-14-59—852
07-77 Geraline, 7-43-58—954
62-43 Gerard, 78-47-62—274
21-62 Gerardo, 15-26-62—402
22-38 Gerda, 57-68-38—838
81-41 Geri, 47-41-31—117
08-12 German, 8-12-2—192
18-43 Geronimo, 5-18-43—-345
18-43 Geronymo, 5-18-43—185
09-30 Gerry, 23-37-30—732
69-48 Gertie, 9-48-24—984
68-69 Gertrude, 19-66-69—166
16-46 Gertrudis, 42-46-16—144
02-77 Gervasio, 4-21-32—221
56-27 Getchen, 52-63-73—063

27-57 Gibbons, 10-27-57—177
27-43 Gibbs, 4-43-68—485
50-86 Gibson, 37-59-62—809
84-69 Gideon, 15-49-60—495
08-45 Giffen, 72-45-15—557
37-95 Gifford, 20-41-30—040
15-59 Gil, 25-36-59—500
15-67 Gilbert, 13-15-67—357
26-85 Gilchrist, 31-62-26—668
35-53 Gilder, 9-11-53—695
05-15 Giles, 5-11-15—515
15-55 Gillespie, 15-20-55—555
44-57 Gilliam, 41-44-57—741
66-99 Gillie, 19-30-42—309
01-71 Gilmore, 51-63-71—136
36-49 Gilp, 61-63-78—663
82-33 Gipson, 8-40-47—408
52-25 Gines, 71-52-25—275
29-94 Ginger, 29-37-56—736
70-07 Giordano, 1-23-37—123
14-44 Giron, 50-60-70—000
43-58 Giuseppe, 18-39-43—938
50-84 Gladays, 60-50-30—563
30-59 Gladien, 5-30-59—178
26-35 Gladner, 27-35-26—537
43-72 Gladys, 8-43-72—547
93-50 Glass, 27-29-30—89
24-38 Gleaton, 70-57-38—357
16-71 Glen, 12-14-16—111
43-84 Glendia, 38-49-60—069
16-72 Glenn, 33-72-59—802
27-59 Glina, 59-70-63—679
51-62 Glora, 17-28-62—827
81-83 Glover, 11-18-27—872
11-51 Gloria, 2-11-51—559
19-60 Godard, 69-60-19—669
28-37 Godfrey, 28-53-59—259
42-72 Godos, 7-58-72—258
06-34 Godoy, 37-48-34—843
12-40 Godwin, 9-12-40—895
09-92 Gold, 5-9-42—592
09-28 Goldberg, 12-28-43—344
13-28 Golden, 12-13-60—792
82-55 Goldfield, 29-65-55—566
23-61 Goldie, 16-27-61—167
21-31 Goldina, 31-21-62—501
19-64 Goldman, 16-22-64—624
59-64 Goldstein, 24-59-67—597

07-75 Goldston, 7-37-75—753
29-99 Golivia, 29-39-49—399
70-77 Golston, 7-70-77—007
41-55 Gomez, 47-53-55—735
46-68 Goncalo, 11-59-68—981
13-31 Goncalves, 55-66-77—567
59-88 Gones, 32-59-62—952
18-85 Gonsalo, 22-68-18—882
23-39 Gonzalez, 4-14-23—413
62-18 Gonzalo, 45-56-67—654
54-65 Goode, 34-54-65—700
53-77 Gooden, 74-77-67—746
54-44 Goodman, 3-54-65—045
13-66 Goolsby, 38-78-66—838
19-49 Gordan, 8-10-49 -906
49-50 Gordon, 14-18-50—360
8-100 Goree, 67-43-14- -346
45-78 Goslin, 13-45-78—450
09-90 Gould, 10-16-9—996
33-60 Grace, 3-46-60—460
27-47 Gracey, 18-27-47—462
58-98 Gracia, 29-57-61—167
99-22 Grade, 2-6-16—126
52-66 Grady, 6-66-35—624
12-22 Grafreed, 48-56-63—583
40-70 Gragirena, 2-5-70—363
01-41 Graham, 23-33-53—653
47-71 Grande, 2-44-47-427
65-89 Grandeza, 37-77-28—877
19-39 Grange, 19-39-47—481
18-19 Granger, 18-71-72—722
04-40 Grant, 4-11-40—444
12-33 Granville, 65-33-51—821
52-83 Grata, 71-56-42—909
55-59 Gratia, 55-59-60—850
11-77 Gratiana, 7-11-77—711
17-49 Graverly, 31-49-58—450
48-97 Graves, 10-33-44—960
52-27 Gray, 23-54-65—450
07-17 Grayson, 7-17-40—963
15-50 Greeley, 15-48-50—483
45-60 Green, 15-45-65—401
45-60 Greene, 5-45-56—041
03-90 Gregorio, 3-19-53—621
03-07 Gregory, 7-8-10—780
68-82 Greta, 8-18-52—761
15-56 Gretchen, 27-49-56—947
05-34 Gretta, 58-73-34—335

14-20 Gricelda, 43-60-70—003
06-26 Griffen, 6-26-53—790
57-64 Griffie, 13-59-64—649
33-65 Griffin, 33-54-65—503
53-65 Griffith, 35-53-65—300
74-08 Griggs, 17-36-74—367
09-30 Grimes, 3-9-30—309
23-30 Grimm, 18-23-30—302
32-69 Griselda, 12-33-69—931
37-61 Gross, 17-33-61—003
52-78 Grossman, 52-36-78—005
95-30 Grover, 45-67-33-490
06-40 Groves, 5-46-54—564
27-86 Grubbs, 27-41-50—430
41-45 Guadalupe, 54-66-46—614
54-67 Gualberto, 23-54-67—234
14-94 Guardia, 31-69-41—963
23-60 Guarino, 58-60-75—068
27-38 Guerra, 21-27-38—227
02-22 Guice, 65-45-33—365
32-52 Guillaume, 39-52-64—293
18-87 Guillermo, 3-18-39—813
10-30 Guillen, 30-53-60—030
27-43 Guindo, 75-43-27—347
79-84 Guiñes, 5-22-31—492
29-84 Guinevere, 29-38-44—842
21-61 Gumersindo, 64-60-4—846
37-93 Gunther, 13-56-71—540
18-28 Gurley, 24-28-30—302
51-15 Gumese, 9-15-51—155
42-70 Gus, 52-70-66—765
12-32 Gusman, 20-62-47—267
16-56 Gussie, 3-9-56—195
63-72 Gustave, 15-30-63—335
23-63 Gustavo, 34-63-73—347
36-63 Gustella, 42-18-12—112
40-80 Guthrie, 1-40-52—241
21-61 Gutierrez, 21-31-61—111
36-76 Guy, 4-31-52—523
03-92 Guzman, 76-54-36—576
47-50 Gwen, 51-70-47—071
100-4 Gwendolyn, 28-34-44—482
33-72 Gwingolia, 62-72-67—766
07-11 Gyndolyn, 7-11-54 116

# H

71-17 Hackney, 17-48-57—4-17
26-36 Haddie, 8-24-36—826

| | |
|---|---|
| 13-43 Haddon, 13-43-48—348 | 11-53 Harriett, 9-11-53—675 |
| 13-33 Hadley, 13-33-40—202 | 11-92 Harriette, 57-63-11—637 |
| 24-39 Hagar, 17-19-63—796 | 17-77 Harriman, 17-70-77—470 |
| 62-19 Hager, 7-19-40—661 | 53-81 Harriot, 14-67-16—676 |
| 15-50 Hagood, 14-15-50—499 | 16-53 Harriott, 7-21-49—124 |
| 60-91 Haidee, 41-61-57—611 | 16-26 Harris, 15-41-68—508 |
| 49-73 Hailey, 25-71-73—375 | 19-64 Harrison, 41-52-67—555 |
| 42-77 Haines, 42-27-47—742 | 07-14 Harrold, 7-14-40—401 |
| 07-70 Hairston, 50-60-70—050 | 35-75 Harry, 5-9-45—632 |
| 16-81 Halbert, 61-72-43—347 | 38-22 Hart, 19-21-58—414 |
| 11-77 Hale, 11-47-77—007 | 93-43 Hartso, 30-43-70—043 |
| 28-58 Haley, 5-58-61—561 | 06-66 Harvey, 6-11-66—808 |
| 36-63 Hall, 33-55-76—764 | 59-49 Harvin, 65-60-50—005 |
| 96-39 Hallie, 56-67-39—522 | 12-54 Harwood, 22-31-54—123 |
| 35-45 Halona, 7-14-35—347 | 13-45 Haslop, 13-45-68—132 |
| 04-44 Halseg, 35-42-44—245 | 05-15 Haston, 5-15-19—716 |
| 25-75 Halsell, 51-37-29—410 | 15-65 Hatcher, 11-55-69—580 |
| 07-11 Hamilton, 7-11-77—682 | 22-34 Hathaway, 5-30-34—340 |
| 47-89 Hamlin, 40-47-58—447 | 11-50 Hattan, 11-46-50—115 |
| 11-41 Hammett, 10-11-41—308 | 36-48 Hattie, 49-53-57—881 |
| 12-40 Hammond, 12-31-40—402 | 07-82 Hatton, 23-32-17—713 |
| 12-40 Hammonds, 12-31-40—402 | 76-15 Hawkens, 15-45-60—455 |
| 71-42 Hampton, 8-42-78—489 | 15-45 Hawkins, 15-45-39—478 |
| 69-78 Hancock, 15-69-78—€89 | 06-83 Hay, 6-11-42—395 |
| 22-53 Hand, 71-74-53—174 | 84-75 Hayden, 55-56-75—575 |
| 19-61 Hanentock, 63-61-19—119 | 05-88 Haydon, 26-39-56—936 |
| 04-41 Hanks, 27-55-41—572 | 40-48 Hayes, 21-48-52—821 |
| 16-66 Hanley, 16-61-66—600 | 40-47 Haynes, 21-40-47—403 |
| 25-78 Hannah, 21-46-60—16C | 73-80 Hayward, 4-62-73—634 |
| 14-28 Hannibal, 8-28-67—546 | 25-35 Haywood, 25-35-37—008 |
| 11-51 Hans, 43-56-8—808 | 18-37 Hayworth, 38-76-37—673 |
| 37-73 Hansome, 11-48-73—340 | 32-72 Hazel, 8-19-54—337 |
| 62-47 Happy, 23-45-76-432 | 79-60 Hazelee, 8-19-67—198 |
| 10-33 Hardie, 9-28-33—928 | 24-34 Hazelton, 8-40-34—700 |
| 29-37 Hardiman, 29-37-62—397 | 24-99 Hazelwood, 12-19-54—187 |
| 90-51 Hardy, 14-40-54-452 | 39-59 Heady, 15-39-59—159 |
| 39-59 Hargrove, 35-39-59—499 | 10-30 Heather, 10-30-49—490 |
| 34-46 Hanston, 69-74-34—964 | 98-52 Heber, 53-52-14—553 |
| 53-63 Harlan, 20-56-63—203 | 09-87 Hector, 19-51-66—156 |
| 28-56 Harley, 18-56-72—313 | 29-59 Hedda, 3-10-61—103 |
| 23-46 Harlow, 67-46-12—147 | 03-31 Hedwig, 60-40-31—406 |
| 19-91 Harmodio, 8-29-19—998 | 17-70 Hedy, 24-37-17—177 |
| 12-43 Harmon, 33-43-64—463 | 30-58 Hegwood, 10-30-58—480 |
| 20-74 Haro, 78-74-20—074 | 78-38 Heiner, 74-30-38—304 |
| 14-47 Harold, 18-47-73—597 | 10-14 Heinrich, 2-18-38—882 |
| 14-64 Harper, 14-59-64—432 | 14-29 Heinz, 7-44-4—440 |
| 57-83 Harpin, 8-11-76—198 | 30-41 Helaine, 2-10-51—419 |
| 02-42 Harriet, 48-42-12—122 | 10-18 Helen, 1-21-65—115 |

58-69 Helena, 2-68-69—669
79-97 Heliodora, 52-62-70—070
08-50 Helga, 17-36-50—508
08-45 Heller, 3-45-40—340
40-53 Hemlock, 3-40-53—210
49-69 Hence, 45-56-69—556
39-86 Henderson, 3-46-63—364
20-52 Henley, 20-35-52—163
16-77 Hennie, 11-59-77—951
96-36 Henrene, 5-6-36—207
23-32 Henretta, 12-23-32—232
23-49 Henrietta, 23-49-54—222
13-44 Henrietter, 16-35-44—561
57-68 Henrique, 1-51-57—171
27-40 Henriques, 7-50-67—760
17-20 Henry, 6-17-20—368
45-56 Henson, 13-45-56—560
58-64 Heraelio, 6-17-74—745
14-16 Herbert, 14-15-16—111
58-85 Herlie, 12-15-58—855
32-67 Herman, 44-71-32—720
19-32 Hermanos, 34-72-32—374
56-95 Hermanegildo, 4-6-8—895
11-16 Hermas, 14-44-48—197
47-52 Hermetre, 8-36-52—153
21-76 Hermogenes, 3-7-11—714
100-7 Hernan, 66-77-44—476
01-66 Hernandez, 13-70-66—073
35-55 Hernando, 50-64-55—506
94-42 Hero, 68-42-8—246
28-50 Herrera, 33-73-28—337
22-50 Herrero, 24-58-50—855
06-84 Herschel, 14-75-6—486
14-80 Hershall, 12-21-48—212
46-57 Hert, 41-73-57—374
04-69 Hervey, 30-52-69—250
87-30 Hesslut, 5-65-30—655
22-32 Hester, 22-32-55—711
35-50 Hestner, 35-39-50—350
40-77 Hezekiah, 40-60-77—467
79-49 Hiawatha, 36-49-54—812
23-73 Hibbard, 38-49-73—032
16-19 Hibernia, 14-16-19—199
37-93 Hicks, 60-37-40—736
44-56 Hickson, 20-42-44—444
59-69 Higgins, 10-11-69—333
68-86 High, 74-68-38—884
45-21 Hightower, 45-38-49—557

15-51 Higinio, 12-17-51—186
17-77 Hilaria, 66-75-17—776
17-47 Hilario, 19-53-47—359
06-56 Hilarión, 6-46-56—668
94-62 Hilary, 43-61-54—154
43-78 Hilda, 21-48-32—431
34-15 Hildagard, 15-34-48—158
05-55 Hildagarde, 18-31-54—118
55-67 Hildegard, 3-9-44—934
77-36 Hilderbrand, 7-43-56—537
04-40 Hill, 4-40-47—447
53-67 Hillary, 15-53-67—156
53-67 Hillery, 53-67-71—176
17-78 Hilliard, 4-30-78—004
34-53 Hilliary, 65-34-76—675
15-54 Hiloa, 3-54-78—781
13-40 Hilton, 13-40-53—311
17-77 Hines, 14-17-77—710
23-35 Hinton. 11-35-65—452
11-22 Hipólito, 11-22-63—780
42-66 Hiram, 8-66-35—621
95-09 Hoard, 28-36-44—371
33-66 Hobart, 33-45-57—507
07-17 Hobbs, 6-17-34—322
56-60 Hobson, 22-44-60—460
52-76 Hodge, 8-22-45—582
12-48 Hodges, 12-48-56—401
23-32 Hoffman, 46-23-32—632
47-81 Hogan, 32-55-47—752
06-96 Hogans, 17-62-6—266
16-34 Holden, 67-76-34—741
41-56 Holland, 2-23-41—423
14-40 Holliday, 14-40-50—408
57-75 Hollie, 33-68-57—867
14-51 Hollins, 25-51-31—113
48-89 Hollinsworth, 7-9-44—944
44-97 Holloway, 44-47-54—544
24-49 Holly, 23-56-49—808
20-36 Holman, 3-20-36—366
56-90 Holmes, 5-6-9—590
37-56 Holt, 20-43-56—533
31-58 Holton, 51-64-74—645
63-88 Hombre, 14-29-63—963
34-42 Homer, 58-34-42—761
38-70 Homero, 50-30-20—030
13-45 Hornsby, 13-45-50—905
56-76 Hortense, 11-76-59—198
24-61 Horton, 24-34-54—532

99-67 Hosea, 7-27-67—815
19-49 Hosia, 6-25-8—008
01-91 Hotchkiss, 10-16-55—015
12-32 House, 5-12-32—324
11-44 Houston, 11-44-56—544
83-38 Howard, 15-22-38—595
26-72 Howell, 15-22-45^440
34-42 Hozziz, 11-34-42—328
39-62 Hubbard, 6-12-20—612
15-75 Hubert, 15-33-75—776
11-17 Huberta, 1-11-17—431
49-67 Hudson, 15-49-70—114
63-18 Huerta, 57-78-63—687
10-73 Huerto, 47-71-10—100
28-08 Huesear, 15-35-28—553
40-50 Huff, 11-40-49—411
32-82 Hufton, 32-45-47—509
40-49 Huggins, 40-43-49—490
19-38 Hugh, 19-38-62—570
19-38 Hughes, 19-38-62—582
83-38 Hughey, 10-20-45—501
74-98 Hughlan, 56-70-74—756
54-86 Homes, 63-54-41—146
03-33 Honey, 28-40-33—334
19-29 Honor, 59-29-19—999
13-43 Honora, 13-43-57—431
47-59 Honorable, 4-72-47—724
56-62 Honoria, 27-39-74—965
28-85 Honorria, 49-50-35—852
07-11 Honus, 10-7-11—844
11-77 Hoosier, 44-4-77—407
71-92 Hop, 3-50-68—508
24-35 Hope, 15-35-27—380
12-71 Hopewell, 32-54-56—311
35-78 Hopkins, 35-38-78—008
02-60 Hopson, 38-58-60—685
50-20 Horace, 43-62-71—333
48-84 Horacio, 26-37-51—172
01-10 Horatio, 1-10-56—589
14-27 Hom, 36-48-14—836
63-43 Homer, 10-18-43—433
56-65 Hughley, 15-44-65—543
51-90 Hugo, 1-18-56—816
17-25 Huida, 24-34-17-473
07-33 Huldah, 16-77-7—777
12-64 Huldy, 69-64-52—648
39-14 Hull, 25-39-58-412
55-72 Humbert, 30-47-52—254

36-63 Humberto, 9-20-36—029
44-58 Humes, 18-44-58—808
15-44 Humphrey, 1-15-44—097
54-89 Hunt, 13-43-54—303
27-38 Hunter, 18-38-54—118
14-49 Huntley, 14-30-49—333
45-79 Hural, 40-65-45—460
14-94 Huron, 29-48-14—144
31-69 Hurston, 7-73-69—973
40-72 Hurtado, 46-59-40—729
15-07 Hurten, 18-28-38—888
17-71 Hussey, 5-41-17—147
12-53 Huston, 26-64-12—642
78-25 Hutcherson, 58-43-36—433
38-70 Hutcheson, 29-38-57—403
09-87 Hutchins, 9-40-53—306
09-81 Hutchinson, 9-43-54—401
34-46 Hutton, 12-30-49—320

# I

03-30 Iago, 45-72-60—725
25-95 Ian, 17-27-63—721
30-38 Ibanez, 26-39-58—238
16-69 Ibbie, 16-38-43—732
34-23 Ibérico, 49-34-23—234
61-77 Icabod, 10-16-61—161
50-75 Ida, 50-71-75—505
54-65 Idamae, 71-65-54—389
68-56 Idella, 5-10-55—758
12-70 Idia, 71-60-40—001
06-86 Idonia, 31-42-6—423
90-24 Ignacio, 24-34-41—144
47-57 Ignatia, 25-50-62—527
41-64 Ignatius, 41-53-64—635
34-96 Igoe, 35-45-65—556
27-57 Ike, 62-27-57—276
57-68 Ildefonso, 6-8-58—865
02-20 Ilene, 51-60-22—510
43-22 Ilka, 15-24-37—725
10-76 Imogene, 2-43-10—012
57-85 Ina, 32-57-75—773
24-48 Inalee, 24-50-48—330
58-65 Indalecio, 61-70-65—716
34-57 Ines, 34-54-57—008
35-45 Inez, 51-38-45—782
16-45 Ineza, 16-49-58—160
53-64 Ingersol, 14-53-68—802
35-53 Ingersoll, 35-56-29—559

41-48 Ingle, 32-54-67—467
40-78 Ingleside, 39-48-78—700
05-97 Ingram, 25-37-49—110
21-33 Inigo, 33-44-12—123
67-84 Inona, 14-52-67—514
08-18 Iola, 8-18-66—545
20-26 Iona, 51-39-26—666
12-41 Ira, 12-21-41—777
08-13 Irehne, 39-66-13—963
37-48 Ireland, 15-44-48—140
62-88 Irene, 4-14-41—675
32-80 Iris, 19-57-32—257
35-53 Irish, 35-48-53—401
07-14 Irma, 7-14-28—711
17-71 Irmatine, 71-36-54—817
18-26 Irmina, 38-74-26—274
11-46 Irvin, 5-11-46—006
11-17 Irving, 7-17-57—014
53-04 Irwin, 6-11-43—433
39-46 Isa, 9-35-46—953
60-99 Isaac, 3-11-60—308
37-56 Isaacson, 10-35-56—800
44-51 Isabel, 28-37-44—437
24-93 Isabele, 2-4-10—500
12-36 Isabell, 12-18-36—874
11-12 Isabella, 4-11-19—119
52-61 Isabelle, 75-61-42—164
43-62 Isadora, 31-44-62—371
06-60 Isadore, 6-12-42—804
28-66 Isaiah, 28-63-66—532
37-73 Isaías, 3-21-36—133
16-29 Isan, 56-67-16—676
92-43 Isbel, 3-11-43—343
43-59 Isbella, 10-11-59—701
60-19 Ish, 4-17-38—410
81-43 Isham, 15-43-54—534
43-53 Ishmael, 14-53-58—590
23-43 Isidoro, 32-43-54—440
44-53 Isidro, 5-10-44—438
27-43 Ismael, 35-55-27—535
28-36 Isola, 1-22-36—263
14-54 Isom, 13-14-54—788
66-51 Isora, 33-11-54—742
28-75 Israel, 28-34-75—235
28-44 Israelites, 13-44-46—004
01-74 Isreal, 54-60-74—064
42-82 Ituri, 12-24-42—222
30-37 Iva, 9-37-62—163

35-91 Ivan, 13-45-58—334
59-74 Ivie, 76-38-21—183
11-45 Ivory, 2-11-45—329
23-50 Ivy, 23-26-50—230
50-60 Ixca, 68-60-50—668
15-98 Izara, 34-77-15—743
38-66 Izora, 13-23-38—231

# J

09-20 Jabe, 78-62-53—526
49-19 Jacie, 8-19-49—712
34-75 Jacinto, 53-69-70—695
40-50 Jack, 3-40-50—400
13-26 Jackie, 26-13-40—478
83-38 Jackson, 38-45-54—354
23-68 Jacob, 15-23-56—256
10-30 Jacoba, 3-10-30—808
52-34 Jacobo, 28-51-63—361
24-81 Jacobina, 65-71-59—765
43-53 Jacobs, 13-43-53—330
35-92 Jacobson, 13-35-56—351
66-73 Jacqueline, 59-44-71—022
66-69 Jacques, 69-43-20—023
38-62 Jafar, 12-16-38—381
22-44 Jaime, 3-18-45—318
33-69 Jake, 2-14-69—751
18-80 James, 3-18-45—987
23-43 Jameston, 23-34-43—353
17-53 Jamie, 5-64-53—564
19-69 Jamison, 23-19-36—342
61-91 Jan, 17-75-61—175
10-15 Jane, 5-10-15—155
36-93 Janet, 3-6-9—963
43-79 Janetta, 10-34-42—034
06-36 Janey, 44-49-61—946
24-32 Janice, 27-52-38—825
12-68 Janie, 63-68-42—668
78-83 Janise, 4-16-18—164
39-49 Jannie, 11-39-49—390
57-27 Janula, 56-58-73—857
11-47 Japo, 4-11-47—474
66-73 Jaqueline, 35-13-37—377
90-23 Jardin, 58-63-32—638
14-31 Jarees, 26-72-14—714
42-67 Jarett, 35-67-70—700
32-54 Jarrett, 32-43-54—113
66-77 Jarutha, 76-66-56—656
100-9 Jason, 44-47-59—459

06-66 Jasper, 6-14-66—802
24-47 Javier, 53-58-62—285
19-89 Jay, 45-57-19—975
15-41 Jean, 2-25-41—221
20-55 Jeanetta, 36-20-55—506
33-63 Jeanette, 1-41-63—007
66-99 Jeanne, 73-66-16—739
03-45 Jedediah, 15-62-3—615
67-76 Jeff, 24-54-67—766
22-49 Jeffers, 13-37-22—273
20-30 Jefferson, 56-66-70—765
34-88 Jeffie, 34-44-53—434
34-73 Jeffrey, 34-1-73—378
37-73 Jeffries, 8-11-38—304
10-60 Jemima, 3-10-60—211
42-56 Jeneva, 12-15-26—255
08-10 Jenine, 15-20-40—002
75-18 Jenkens, 17-18-39—319
18-55 Jenkins, 55-71-37—408
04-65 Jenna, 46-55-65—465
16-46 Jennie, 29-77-46—779
27-68 Jennifer, 14-23-38—824
17-29 Jennings, 7-67-17—677
09-21 Jenny, 11-12-43—482
16-21 Jenson, 16-21-40—60
15-18 Jeremiah, 15-18-39—399
25-93 Jeremias, 33-25-63—332
07-82 Jeremy, 6-43-7—746
51-74 Jerica, 59-74-66—954
15-18 Jerimiah, 15-18-39—399
70-82 Jerline, 70-60-40—000
26-67 Jerome, 45-67-21—823
2-100 Jeronimo, 42-50-57—424
35-67 Jerry, 3-55-49—411
02-61 Jess, 18-32-46—681
13-94 Jesse, 15-36-59—003
50-74 Jessell, 34-74-76—008
51-61 Jessica, 51-61-46—461
37-66 Jessie, 10-7-66—824
31-83 Jessye, 15-43-8—909
26-44 Jesus, 3-19-26—939
36-59 Jethroe, 11-16-39—819
08-71 Jetine, 31-49-38—841
27-60 Jett, 11-32-78—332
80-16 Jettie, 15-45-65—562
26-39 Jewel, 8-19-61—817
01-95 Jewell, 5-19-45—780
49-84 Jewett, 17-37-78—800

52-77 Jezabel, 52-41-39—869
28-88 Jill, 60-78-28—067
37-77 Jimenez, 41-37-77—143
18-59 Jimmie, 3-18-45—987
18-45 Jimmy, 45-52-61—524
56-57 Jincy, 7-13-57—010
96-72 Joab, 20-74-62—742
11-13 Joan, 11-13-56—113
27-89 Joanna, 48-69-14—489
27-85 Joanne, 9-19-27—199
15-90 Joaquin, 30-40-15—043
48-58 Joaquina, 1-21-31—111
40-68 Job, 10-14-68—106
11-21 Jocelin, 21-33-57—332
11-21 Jocelyn, 33-21-11—312
38-61 Joe, 61-68-38—668
09-15 Joel, 9-15-62—916
73-63 Johan, 39-47-70—479
97-66 Johanna, 66-26-73—717
31-57 John, 31-56-75—357
57-47 Johanna, 15-43-58—393
20-86 Johnella, 8-22-12—212
28-31 John Henry, 51-31-4—171
16-27 Johnie, 11-16-40—901
06-66 Johnnie, 6-66-70—606
07-17 Johnny, 7-17-63—808
39-98 Johnson, 26-36-49—811
26-34 Johnston, 26-34-57—400
36-64 Johnstone, 36-48-49—400
47-58 Jonah, 16-44-58—459
87-40 Jonas, 6-48-40—311
05-29 Jonathon, 5-6-25—565
40-50 Jones, 14-40-50—003
26-75 Joplin, 15-26-75—570
87-50 Jordan, 8-9-50—122
26-50 Jordenia, 8-17-26—260
52-75 Jorge, 12-34-75—377
14-34 foscos, 20-28-49—289
63-77 Jose, 44-63-77—364
24-42 Josef, 13-33-66—313
08-74 Josefa, 52-61-16—665
51-95 Josefina, 9-21-34—219
18-35 Joseph, 18-35-62—336
72-14 Josepha, 72-76-61—776
16-62 Josephine, 7-10-11—710
18-55 Josephs, 18-55-68—488
35-80 Josephus, 78-40-21—408
46-59 Joshua, 18-46-59—869

32-64 Josiah, 56-64-66—666
45-50 Josie, 22-45-50—452
25-86 Joy, 60-25-10—010
39-60 Joyce, 2-39-53—393
52-61 Juan, 71-74-52—277
52-73 Juana, 43-52-73—325
18-52 Juanita, 18-52-61—809
36-71 Judah, 51-59-71—195
46-73 Judge, 15-73-75—379
56-60 Judith, 11-56-60—600
94-15 Judson, 5-7-9—955
14-44 Judy, 23-44-14—412
60-49 Julanie, 8-34-70—704
09-99 Jules, 14-24-9—914
12-17 Julia, 2-6-17—617
31-58 Julian, 31-58-72—178
17-31 Juliana, 6-17-31—716
26-99 Julie, 58-77-26—857
38-63 Juliette, 8-15-63—810
37-83 Juline, 13-33-37—333
16-70 Julio, 35-50-70—005
04-14 Julius, 4-14-67—303
47-75 Julues, 25-47-75—742
48-56 June, 19-17-56-435
56-72 Junge, 69-72-56—972
38-93 Junípero, 42-38-16—834
10-59 Junius, 7-26-59—726
34-84 Jusepe, 76-38-44—438
02-20 Justin, 15-36-20—635
27-69 Justiniano, 7-9-43—979
17-47 Justine, 57-68-47—865
58-98 Justo, 15-58-60—558

# K

43-58 Kansas, 8-16-58—110
10-21 Kantor, 4-35-50—400
35-45 Kaplan, 35-54-69—568
39-68 Karan, 39-14-68—329
18-85 Karen, 37-56-68—376
72-92 Karl, 16-27-72—772
28-68 Karla, 6-49-67—946
03-57 Kasey, 41-75-57—714
15-35 Kate, 15-35-61—569
35-66 Kates, 19-55-66—876
53-64 Katharen, 45-53-64—354
07-23 Katharine, 12-3248—231
88-33 Katherina, 20-62-33—622
13-66 Katherine, 34-6649—903

43-73 Kathleen, 8-10-68—680
81-96 Kathrine, 26-14-10—112
10-13 Kathryn, 4-10-50—110
100-6 Kathryne, 11-46-6—664
32-43 Kathy, 3-31-43—331
22-34 Katie, 63-73 34—333
14-44 Katlin, 19-44-50—322
13-89 Katrina, 8-13-41—143
44-88 Katy, 10-4044—040
09-19 Kauffman, 9-19-46—770
39-58 Kaufman, 26-39-59—399
39-79 Kay, 54-70-39—705
06-41 Kea, 39-64-41-649
01-65 Kean, 1-30-65—316
60-77 Keaton, 1-11-77—665
31-54 Kee, 19-31-45—931
17-65 Keefe, 10-17-65—552
82-67 Keefer, 945-67—681
13-32 Keeley, 13-3245—345
45-38 Keep, 19-38-2—138
06-16 Keith, 6-16-56—459
12-21 Kellar, 21-36-59—456
13-60 Kelly, 9-16-60—960
78-39 Kemp, 54-39-45—620
29-39 Ken, 5-29-36—081
66-36 Kendall, 12-36-42—124
43-56 Kennedy, 43-56-29—452
15-56 Kenneth, 10-15-56—009
16-66 Kent, 10-16-66—163
14-44 Kenzie, 4-14-44—532
20-40 Kester, 74-40-2—274
55-90 Kevelin, 29-47-55—749
41-46 Kevin, 5-18-36—851
05-67 Keziah, 38-55-67—386
30-70 Kiah, 65-30-20—025
91-55 Kibby, 5-10-55—876
79-97 Kidd, 16-24-64—644
11-77 Kiders, 28-48-77—788
08-18 Kilbourne, 8-18-66—886
11-69 Kildare, 9-11-69—778
19-56 Kilgore, 17-66-56—667
22-48 Kilian, 2-22-48—443
39-17 Killibrew, 8-17-69—001
17-74 Killigrew, 18-74-69—201
13-50 Killings, 10-16-50—173
08-13 Killjoy, 11-31-66—111
11-50 Kilpatrick, 4-11-50—543
29-52 Kincaid, 11-52-65—831

04-54 King, 6-34-54—501  
59-06 Kingston, 27-38-53—311  
10-06 Kinney, 10-45-66—163  
18-52 Kirby, 19-27-52—901  
12-21 Kirk, 12-21-65—562  
06-12 Kirkland, 6-32-48—843  
18-31 Kirkpatrick, 18-31-54—653  
05-53 Kiri, 2-19-53—682  
07-17 Kiser, 7-17-57—090  
26-69 Kitchrell, 11-19-66—645  
13-33 Kittrell, 14-56-69—356  
29-49 Kitty, 29-49-57—002  
77-57 Klein, 7-57-43—442  
40-51 Klem, 8-38-49—562  
34-62 Klien, 19-45-62—903  
52-67 Knight, 8-27-52—186  
60-04 Knola, 9-27-52—021  
52-56 Knott, 6-10-56—805  
56-72 Knowles 7-56-72—440  
41-65 Knox, 4-41-65—886  
78-91 Kondakor, 21-37-5—454  
35-70 Kostner, 35-43-59—55  
32-68 Kreiger, 13-49-68—333  
28-83 Kresge, 36-38-67—677  
10-20 Kress, 10-20-48—428  
16-69 Kriss, 4-32-69—664  
10-52 Kurtz, 7-10-55—720  
33-66 Kyle, 6-19-66—553  

# L

43-34 Laban, 8-15-64—632  
07-17 Labelle, 7-17-47—912  
56-03 Lacalle, 3-33-56—333  
31-61 Laflin, 11-31-66—166  
71-77 Lagree, 43-65-77—880  
32-42 Lala, 20-31-42—240  
29-85 Lamar, 17-39-29—997  
29-31 Lambert, 11-29-31—139  
24-99 Lambie, 46-56-62—654  
57-67 Lamont, 56-67-57—579  
14-65 Lampkin, 7-14-65—560  
14-41 Lancaster, 7-14-41—321  
35-53 Lance, 2-56-71—650  
71-96 Lancelot, 57-72-60—725  
22-62 Landeen, 40-49-62—944  
16-37 Landon, 16-37-56—450  
02-62 Landrum, 9-16-62—662  
16-50 Landry, 3-21-55—532  

37-70 Lane, 45-67-70—330  
36-86 Laney, 25-38-43—344  
43-92 Langston, 29-19-43—919  
12-64 Lapena, 40-78-64—406  
63-85 Laplin, 14-17-19—197  
54-72 Lara, 41-58-72—281  
50-58 Larabee, 32-50-58—182  
40-82 Larentia, 50^66-71—506  
10-44 Larina, 4-32-44—443  
23-73 Larine, 34-73-23—234  
27-78 Larissa, 21-27-37—717  
26-58 Larrea, 33-49-58—466  
18-66 Larry, 66-18-43—717  
41-76 Laso, 8-65-41—685  
19-58 Lasso, 30-71-58—958  
05-59 Lateena, 9-5-59—018  
22-66 Latice, 22-64-66—622  
07-68 Latifa, 29-70-68—709  
12-90 Laucinda, 3-12-34—213  
50-73 Lauderdale, 72-73-68—48⌐  
37-95 Launcelot, 2-37-54—452  
25-48 Laur, 69-48-25—584  
68-75 Laura, 15-68-75—751  
39-84 Lauree, 19-28-39—899  
17-49 Laureen, 2-64-17^62  
32-78 Laurel, 38-48-32—843  
67-75 Lauren, 11-18-67—678  
38-43 Laurene, 1-38-43—438  
26-79 Laurence, 1-55-75—703  
20-89 Laurice, 55-78-20—002  
39-70 Laurette, 27-63-70—736  
11-22 Lavender, 1-37-11—111  
14-44 LaVergne, 55-27-13—133  
48-98 Laverne, 47-54-48—547  
13-31 Lavemia, 77-31-20—713  
49-94 Laverta, 13-26-49—623  
26-57 Lavina, 45-68-26—864  
21-47 Lavinia, 7-25-47—547  
38-66 Lavonia, 62-66-30—630  
13-25 Lawler, 3-25-38—382  
15-49 Lawndale, 15-49-59—409  
33-63 Lawrence, 55-56-63—533  
48-69 Lawson, 48-50-69—703  
88-80 Lawton, 10-14-20—014  
08-47 Lax, 53-76-47—763  
30-41 Layman, 44-61-41—614  
56-60 Layton, 24-37-60—502  
48-79 Lazaro, 36-48-69—846

48-53 Lazarus, 48-53-57—573
41-48 Lea, 41-48-50—004
09-90 Leachman, 33-40-9—135
22-37 Leah, 52-37-22—735
4-100 Leander, 15-21-14—125
14-93 Leandro, 43-75-49—573
100-3 Leaner, 6-24-3—246
26-46 Leanna, 67-46-26—666
38-65 Leaper, 60-65-38—508
01-81 Learlener, 41-52-63—325
50-97 Leatha, 51-60-21—165
55-66 Leathers, 74-66-55—567
07-57 Leatrice, 7-57-48—080
37-87 Leavell 35-42-37—253
45-74 Leclaire, 59-74-45—749
15-45 Ledon, 5-22-45—225
64-72 Ledy, 23-64-72—462
50-71 Lee, 32-50-71—641
23-49 Legrand, 36-49-68—877
03-69 Leigh, 44-69-33—369
42-77 Leila, 22-12-42—222
56-88 Leinder, 6-56-66—568
47-52 Leia, 7-47-52—912
25-59 Lelah, 23-37-25—973
38-42 Lelia, 14-18-38—814
42-57 Lelola, 34-57-42—427
18-39 Lemarah, 2-43-39—324
89-97 Lemos, 68-66-40—686
33-48 Lemuel, 30-48-33—340
39-51 Len, 1-39-51—915
23-69 Lena, 15-69-48—090
40-70 Lenell, 27-40-70—007
4-100 Lenese, 22-34-44—434
10-78 Lenise, 33-78-10—108
52-60 Lenita, 58-60-52—256
63-90 Lennie, 78-12-63—217
16-78 Lennox, 13-16-78—613
64-59 Lenora, 42-33-59—334
27-98 Lenore, 21-32-27—231
43-79 Leo, 69-43-11—149
10-16 Leola, 4-10-16—517
43-34 Leon, 2-12-34—800
34-45 Leona, 57-71-45—012
34-27 Leonard, 16-27-50—507
34-58 Leonardo, 22-34-58—109
15-71 Leonidas, 12-59-71—115
26-61 Leonora, 41-45-61—466
34-99 Leonore, 70-34-12—703

28-73 Leopold, 51-73-55—557
80-86 Leopoldo, 20-30-40-000
44-91 Leora, 20-60-44—294
20-40 Leota, 31-71-20—341
99-09 Lerin, 46-56-69—566
14-40 Lodell, 3-58-14—853
21-11 Lerleine, 11-40-21—114
44-27 Leroy, 44-15-62—310
63-52 Lesa, 36-47-25—365
12-27 Leslie, 7-27-56—444
19-99 Lessie, 41-40-38—998
08-48 Lester, 5-8-48—901
34-62 Letha, 61-72-34—617
35-39 Letite, 23-35-39—408
18-45 Letitia, 4-15-18—181
43-72 Lettice, 14-43-72—143
56-35 Lettie, 19-47-56—910
53-81 Letty, 30-53-64—503
28-92 Leua, 73-28-9—827
19-79 Level, 10-62-19—611
46-94 Levela, 39-46-49—449
87-68 Levella, 12-11-10—100
41-14 Levena, 4-14-44—144
37-73 Levenia, 48-74-37—784
02-82 Levester, 5-49-2—952
50-63 Levi, 63-16-50—016
54-29 Levine, 18-29-54—592
36-48 Levolia, 6-8-48—326
29-39 Levy, 51-39-45—827
19-87 Lew, 56-66-19—689
39-49 Lewellyn, 28-39-49—477
33-96 Lewgean, 27-33-47—723
47-57 Lewis, 52-47-57—277
54-68 Lian, 14-56-68—211
76-86 Liane, 9-35-76—935
43-58 Libby, 56-43-78—632
32-68 Libertad, 67-32-23—419
17-24 Licenciado, 3-7-17—737
39-69 Lida, 55-39-69—690
09-39 Lidia, 2-59-9—950
26-39 Lidya, 24-55-39—542
04-50 Lige, 32-38-56—588
19-38 Liggett, 19-38-56—601
29-48 Lightfoot, 29-48-64—463
11-41 Lila, 12-46-54—831
01-57 Lilar, 15-66-18—665
85-67 Lili, 36-54-45—453
43-75 Lilian, 8-25-43—852

61-95 Lillian, 61-14-55—814
40-84 Lillie, 77-40-68—047
31-56 Lilly, 1-4-10—107
18-38 Lillydale, 18-38-58—888
23-49 Lilo, 53-65-49—659
66-77 Lily, 39-77-9—371
30-50 Lilybell, 11-30-50—502
12-22 Lincoln, 18-19-22—161
56-39 Linda, 31-46-72—814
14-19 Lindbergh, 14-18-19—109
01-11 Lindolfo, 1-11-59—431
17-28 Lindsay, 11-28-49—390
28-43 Lindsey, 28-43-56—455
12-22 Lindy, 7-52-76—752
35-05 Liner, 26-37-30—307
24-28 Link, 24-28-39—311
42-74 Linnie, 4-6-9—755
13-48 Linsey, 5-13-48—496
67-56 Lionel, 2-37-56—237
38-48 Lipscomb, 6-14-57—577
40-58 Liria, 40-58-67—933
26-57 Lisa, 30-57-8—356
43-65 Lisandro, 4-43-65—644
37-06 Lisette, 38-64-37—683
21-93 Lita, 16-27-21—271
24-07 Little, 24-37-64—433
07-83 Littlejohn, 51-62-77—627
21-23 Littles, 20-21-23—303
21-34 Littleton, 4-34-57—490
55-69 Livert, 46-56-69—540
13-30 Livia, 23-43-46—466
20-37 Livingston, 20-32-54—441
07-11 Livingstone, 7-11-50—404
14-47 Liza, 50-75-47—744
08-64 Lizardi, 17-28-8—080
54-29 Lizette, 16-50-54—556
02-74 Lizie, 38-67-74—476
42-17 Lizzetta, 71-74-67—677
64-38 Lizzie, 10-38-64—830
12-21 Lizzy, 24-54-61—154
47-87 Llewellyn, 59-7-4—974
08-18 Lloyd, 8-18-33—518
35-81 Locke, 10-20-35—102
30-48 Lockett, 29-30-48—447
4-100 Locust, 18-36-65—400
31-55 Lody, 33-55-62—551
39-98 Lodyster, 4-7-9—001
47-57 Loehrs, 14-57-72—507

28-58 Logan, 28-35-58—93
52-66 Lois, 66-54-71—352
59-65 Lola, 8-11-59—187
03-33 Loleta, 3-33-39—331
33-63 Lolita, 29-41-63—708
22-79 Lollie, 5-10-55—734
27-47 Lombard, 6-31-47—114
33-75 Lona, 6-13-33—312
40-58 London, 19-37-58—002
30-40 Loney, 73-62-40-004
45-69 Long, 20-45-69—455
56-71 Lonnie, 60-56-66—765
40-88 Lonny, 25-40-61—425
30-51 Lope, 51-63-69—008
12-66 Lopez, 8-12-39—408
03-57 Lora, 57-64-75—675
46-23 Lorain, 39-46-57—693
76-89 Loraine, 7-10-56—534
19-89 Lorelei, 57-75-18—575
82-95 Lorelia, 24-3-28—849
18-24 Lorena, 11-74-23—317
23-15 Lorene, 45-23-15—584
46-67 Lorenia, 49-67-48—602
39-49 Lorenza, 27-39-54—173
94-49 Lorenzo, 15-49-38—606
21-37 Loretta, 21-45-37—332
30-41 Lori, 61-30-41—130
26-31 Loria, 17-26-31—671
89-24 Lorna, 56-75-66—576
48-67 Lorraine, 4-40-48—844
04-82 Lorren, 34-46-44—643
58-77 Lossie, 68-77-55—778
47-38 Lotice. 20-38-47—498
46-61 Lott, 46-69-78—433
68-90 Lotta, 27-33-68—323
29-59 Lottie, 12-29-59—299
32-83 Lotty, 47-62-65—647
63-96 Lou, 14-83-91—493
09-49 Loue, 5-35-55—555
42-53 Louella, 76-53-42—376
64-79 Louida, 15-20-33—586
16-76 Louie, 18-28-76—881
27-37 Louis, 3-11-37—317
94-79 Louisa, 36-42-59—531
51-94 Louise, 7-51-63—559
60-80 Louisiana, 20-40-60—246
37-71 Lourita, 22-71-38—108
33-53 Louvella, 72-53-33—372

28-19 Louvenia, 11-19-27—117
19-34 Louvinia, 19-23-54—004
07-37 Louwanna, 51-15-37—555
27-63 Lova, 32-63-72—363
10-20 Love, 5-10-20—200
14-40 Loveana, 14-29-39—396
86-06 Lovejoy, 66-06-26—600
20-73 Lovett, 33-20-45—420
13-46 Loveone, 9-49-51—159
52-62 Lovetta, 44-71-52-744
32-54 Lovewell, 32-37-54—003
09-19 Lovie, 9-19-56—405
18-39 Lowden, 18-39-58—533
36-50 Lowe, 8-39-50—510
19-27 Lowell, 9-38-47—477
40-50 Lowie, 23-40-50—703
52-14 Lowry, 17-52-58—522
27-45 Loza, 2-28-37—702
24-44 Lucas, 24-44-66—500
81-99 Lucia, 22-33-55—352
42-12 Lucian, 31-78-60—871
72-79 Luciano, 2-65-72—623
01-86 Luciel, 15-48-19—938
16-61 Lucila, 8-37-61—178
93-10 Lucile, 43-52-58—554
18-35 Lucille, 8-12-59—218
04-12 Lucinda, 4-19-12—781
26-51 Lucinder, 70-30-51—731
39-64 Lucius, 12-51-64—214
28-71 Luckett, 64-52-43—645
11-33 Luckie, 11-21-33—321
08-11 Lucky, 52-42-11—524
11-23 Lucretia, 11-23-38—123
10-80 Lucy, 10-16-44—441
44-59 Lucy Belle, 4-8-12—898
67-82 Luddie, 14-16-8—161
36-92 Ludia, 30-69-73—379
50-69 Ludie, 50-52-69—355
27-46 Ludwig, 27-35-46—247
50-62 Lue, 20-31-62—613
21-47 Lueberda, 12-21-47—112
17-71 Luella, 7-20-17—717
100-6 Luetta, 4-6-16—664
58-59 Luevinia, 7-25-47—547
25-51 Lugenia, 41-53-66—654
69-78 Luhis, 23-60-78—608
31-60 Luis, 63-51-42—251
43-78 Luisa, 13-77-43—731

03-84 Luke, 3-39-45—334
05-91 Lula, 29-36-50—053
33-70 Lulita, 6-16-33—613
12-16 Lulu, 16-36-51—782
39-43 Lumia, 19-54-39—994
07-70 Lummie, 7-10-70—466
24-44 Lumpkin, 46-77-44—477
44-30 Lumpkins, 4-44-30—311
17-74 Luna, 68-74-36—648
35-91 Lupercio, 12-53-35—553
16-09 Lurister, 7-16-9—116
72-81 Lurrey, 76-72-41-427
25-64 Lustress, 38-61-64—183
34-67 Luther, 34-67-49—117
16-64 Lutiel, 16-36-64—636
13-31 Lutitia, 45-31-13—334
42-73 Luttie, 67-73-42—207
30-42 Luvanger, 6-42-30—004
100-2 Luvenia, 10-16-37—763
15-39 Lyde, 15-39-12—625
60-90 Lydia, 37-52-60—605
36-80 Lyle, 21-36-56—532
33-53 Lyles, 60-53-33—603
56-68 Lyman, 30-49-56—554
41-68 Lynch, 48-58-68—669
18-81 Lynette, 5-18-38—881
07-63 Lynn, 75-63-7—657
03-99 Lyons, 13-33-3—333
72-79 Lythia, 10-66-72—279
37-43 Lytie, 44-37-15—153
05-55 Lytle, 5-6-55—455

# M

52-89 Ma, 36-59-52—956
26-31 Mabel, 27-51-31—115
15-59 Mabelle, 15-46-59—466
14-37 Mabie, 14-37-8—766
11-33 Mabry, 11-33-54 444
33-59 Mac, 1-15-59—500
59-78 Macaya, 25-77-78—478
37-62 MacDonald, 27-37-5—157
19-67 Mace, 42-54-67—843
11-30 Maceo, 3-11-30—727
44-67 Macias, 30-58-67—766
06-16 Mack, 6-16-56—699
78-35 Mackay, 35-49-58—401
35-59 Mackey, 11-24-59—321
35-56 Mackie, 32-56-77—878

40-18 Macoy, 3-15-18—883
21-27 Macy, 15-49-58—413
24-32 Madden, 24-38-59—444
04-61 Maddie, 18-25-35—355
16-35 Maddox, 5-35-57-455
30-98 Madelene, 8-30-56—255
20-38 Madelia, 58-63-38—836
15-69 Madeline, 15-69-74—741
67-51 Madelon, 26-35-51—155
11-45 Madendia, 4-14-74—741
17-47 Madge, 7-17-47—970
83-16 Madia, 2-16-32—153
06-16 Madie, 6-16-32—606
88-71 Madison, 12-36-49—490
18-48 Madora, 8-18-48—386
24-65 Madre, 30-40-65-4-03
21-31 Madrid, 19-69-21—112
47-54 Mae, 39-47-54—573
36-08 Magdalena, 3-8-36—680
39-82 Magdalene, 29-54-39—945
34-75 Magee, 18-34-57—467
64-46 Magg, 62-46-26—246
31-23 Maggie, 6-31-45—642
29-92 Maggy, 19-29-39—999
11-71 Magnolia, 2-11-59—171
40-66 Magnus, 41-40-38—834
17-22 Mahaley, 17-22-41—835
11-21 Mahalia, 78-56-11—115
83-55 Maimón, 11-20-55—521
12-26 Maisie, 18-48-26—684
02-93 Maker, 12-24-2—242
16-37 Malachi, 28-37-16—173
29-92 Malafaias, 2-40-51—142
18-67 Malaga, 70-67-18—768
07-77 Malcolm, 7-10-77—112
34-14 Malcom, 28-30-39—003
06-22 Malendia, 63-22-6—226
56-99 Maliano, 17-56-24—564
34-84 Malicia, 21-31-34—332
10-52 Malinda, 4-10-52—918
29-94 Malisa, 55-29-15—159
56-64 Malisha, 14-39-64—270
45-50 Malissa, 45-31-76—650
33-46 Mallie, 49-71-40—079
43-85 Mallory, 75-43-39—003
48-68 Malone, 1-22-48—842
27-76 Malsena, 41-30-27—734
01-11 Malvina, 32-50-11—152

57-95 Marne, 10-50-57—557
09-29 Mamie, 9-29-37—861
36-86 Mammie, 26-36-47—436
14-41 Manda, 14-18-41—181
29-69 Mande, 9-23-99—639
96-10 Mandy, 56-64-40-446
49-52 Manley, 16-43-49—934
21-36 Mann, 72-36-21—213
33-47 Manning, 33-54-69—900
29-58 Mannings, 20-29-30—092
54-59 Manns, 54-59-8—332
51-75 Manos, 51-43-75—223
30-70 Manrique, 24-30-40—434
40-50 Manse, 42-40-50—244
33-42 Mansillas, 8-57-42—758
18-28 Manuel, 33-65-28—862
28-87 Manuela, 20-28-78—722
05-77 Marc, 25-73-77—377
60-74 Marcelino, 15-25-60—605
39-97 Marcell, 30-39-42—290
15-65 Marcella, 34-65-15—123
23-78 Marcelle, 13-73-78—787
31-61 Marcelo, 65-37-31—173
08-68 Marcelous, 3-16-68—361
46-53 March, 29-46-53—465
14-97 Marcia, 59-46-14—149
17-71 Marcial, 18-46-14—149
43-91 Marco, 37-43-57—003
22-36 Marcos, 28-36-42-463
48-51 Marcus, 51-6048—777
39-59 Marcy, 2-10-11—100
27-86 Marea, 48-27-36—276
42-60 Margaret, 9-19-60—906
77-17 Margarette, 18-7643—332
16-60 Margarita, 43-17-7—143
15-32 Margella, 36-58-32—273
19-29 Margery, 18-19-29-465
19-89 Marghuerita, 4-12-10—987
11-17 Margie, 7-11-17—108
27-41 Margot, 47-66-41—167
47-79 Margreat, 74-69-47—496
16-60 Marguerieta, 4-16-72—164
39-70 Marguerita, 16-4-39—941
16-39 Marguerite, 4-8-32—284
62-26 Margurite, 274-62—667
16-43 Margy, 16-23-43—316
92-29 Mari, 35-42-29—945
14-44 Maria, 22-44-64-464

37-87 Marian, 46-57-68—754
02-22 Marianne, 9-57-22—277
25-80 Mariano, 20-25-70—520
54-69 Maribel, 19-39-69—699
24-73 Marice, 10-20-24—201
48-29 Marido, 75-56-48—465
44-18 Marie, 55-69-77—697
26-72 Marietta, 26-37-72—273
17-71 Marigold, 8-45-71—106
39-93 Marilla, 56-59-39—955
42-63 Marilyn, 26-67-74—726
17-20 Marina, 1-20-66—130
40-57 Mario, 3440-57-443
20-66 Marion, 1-20-66—066
36-59 Maris, 24-36-59—364
44-14 Marissa, 55-66-77—675
18-88 Marita, 43-27-38—837
03-55 Marjorie, 8-58-77—420
49-98 Mamia, 1449-68—891
28-34 Mark, 6-20-34—396
34-53 Marks, 8-32-53—331
30-25 Marla, 44-33-25—344
64-73 Marlena, 20-60-64—462
81-18 Marlene, 3-33-65—860
10-88 Mario, 68-51-43—377
94-64 Marlon, 76-26-64—627
04-36 Marquesa, 7-17-44—414
41-56 Marquez, 25-33-39—935
26-11 Marsha, 43-55-11—155
46-49 Marshall, 49-59-46—710
29-81 Marta, 29-37-40—441
21-37 Martha, 11-21-37—111
24-40 Martin, 19-24-40—124
14-34 Martina, 14-34-43—133
09-77 Martine, 24-38-77—837
65-70 Martinez, 6-49-65—946
85-60 Martinho, 38-65-60—066
11-54 Martini, 11-32-54—441
13-99 Martins, 12-13-16—131
45-69 Martz, 30-64-69—943
96-30 Marva, 17-30-42—247
07-70 Marvin, 7-10-70—223
38-90 Marty, 72-78-65—568
19-44 Mary, 19-23-57—193
21-84 Marya, 23-21-48—213
01-52 Maryland, 2-12-52—225
39-59 Marylyn, 11-33-39—913
16-32 Mason, 16-32-48—868

26-76 Massien, 39-26-76—680
44-68 Masterson, 13-50-49—448
18-47 Mateo, 63-71-47—717
18-38 Mathias, 8-18-38—888
28-50 Mathilda, 6-16-28—612
35-30 Mathis, 16-30-59—114
35-46 Matias, 9-35-46—103
66-78 Matilda, 31-50-78—310
06-29 Matilde, 8-45-62—711
67-77 Matthew, 31-32-77—377
28-43 Matthews, 2-43-65—404
32-61 Mattie, 32-61-53—824
37-49 Mattox, 9-36-49—001
56-83 Maud, 12-77-56—771
33-51 Maude, 31-33-51—133
31-37 MaudeU, 10-20-31—201
12-20 Maudella, 18-20-23—432
46-58 Maul, 22-51-58—862
20-43 Maura, 40-62-43—467
16-75 Maure, 1-11-16—115
28-66 Maureen, 70-66-28—876
39-54 Maurella, 27-39-54-493
23-45 Maurice, 23-45-67—552
100-1 Maurine, 52-63-11—136
12-22 Maurita, 15-41-22—245
39-89 Maurya, 77-66-39—766
35-40 Max, 1140-35—541
40-50 Maxie, 35-50-40—817
40-47 Máxime, 61-4047—040
39-95 Maximilian, 3-5-7—732
34-82 Maximiliano, 5-15-34—351
40-65 Maximo, 53-65-70—065
11-66 Maxine, 6-11-66—769
05-11 Maxwell, 5-11-45-451
28-57 Maxyne, 69-57-28—875
19-42 May, 21-54-42—249
27-35 Maybelle, 32-3542—352
30-50 Mayberry, 50-30-8—430
56-74 Mayer, 16-56-74—765
30-56 Mayes, 30-54-56—411
06-66 Mayetta, 6-19-66—743
68-45 Mayfield, 5-10-18—511
22-64 Mayme, 22-50-64—465
53-59 Maynard, 32-42-59—115
43-83 Maynor, 43-54-69—418
12-37 Mayo, 12-25-37—248
12-91 Mays, 34-12-48—554
24-58 Mazola, 3748-58—310

11-67 Mazie, 11-39-59— 433
76-09 Mazzie, 34-45-67—861
27-67 McAlpin, 1947-50—398
36-78 McBrady, 38-48-78—100
17-19 McBride, 4-43-59—908
36-84 McCall, 18-3648—584
36-04 McCarrael, 14-36-59—864
40-44 McCay, 6-19-38—331
21-39 McClary, 18-28-39—003
48-75 McClinton, 3148-56—113
52-66 McCollan, 30-49-57—431
34-44 McGow, 19-34-44—480
20-26 McCoy, 20-35-54-474
56-31 McCrae, 31-54-65—642
10-70 McCrary, 14-18-38—388
29-54 McCray, 29-38-54—889
39-58 McDaniel, 39-53-65—550
16-35 McDaniels, 13-49-57—311
24-48 McDaugall, 24-28-48—488
77-92 McDavid, 42-64-22—221
07-11 McDearmon, 7-11-47—877
43-13 McDonald, 5-13-43—544
10-20 McDuff, 10-20-48—209
25-85 McFarland, 12-36-77—143
29-36 McGee, 19-36-65—433
05-74 McGowan, 14-39-58—38
38-32 McGuire, 1-11-8—998
32-54 McKenzie, 32-54-78—904
46-65 McKinley, 46-76-68—677
39-51 McKinney, 39-47-65—763
65-56 McKire, 18-34-56—008
8-100 McLead, 14-54-63—341
27-64 McLemore, 13-53-64—873
24-93 McNeal, 29-49-56—594
100-6 Meadows, 5-39-66—693
07-15 Means, 68-77-15—761
29-57 Meartz, 13-58-29—853
33-46 Med, 78-46-33—647
86-57 Medley, 21-50-57—051
02-72 Medlock, 30-40-72—003
26-76 Melanie, 69-76-26—669
21-72 Melba, 21-60-72—508
24-64 Melchor, 41-64-14—614
59-42 Melicent, 6-59-42—956
94-73 Melinda, 14-22-73—376
37-23 Melissa, 60-70-37—704
07-50 Meliton, 8-31-51—151
28-82 Mell, 4-12-38—124

03-37 Mellien, 48-57-67—767
54-35 Mellville, 31-35-48-486
18-69 Melone, 19-36-48—411
35-75 Melton, 18-35-75—004
68-42 Melvin, 7-42-64—649
60-84 Melvina, 6-1942—824
29-90 Mendez, 28-29-33—983
99-79 Mendoza, 11-20-67—620
27-38 Menendez, 3747-38—478
08-38 Mennen, 13-49-8—864
81-18 Mercedes, 19-56-66—591
46-67 Mercedier, 3-66-67—673
28-78 Mercer, 7-43-78—808
46-98 Merchant, 35-43-65—732
55-70 Mercy, 1-18-37—401
36-71 Meredith, 36-37-78—432
43-66 Meriam, 6-9-14—614
12-36 Merill, 12-36-75—655
61-70 Meris, 46-77-61—174
20-30 Merle, 18-27-55—567
08-38 Merlin, 21-18-38—881
19-89 Merrill, 10-36-19—936
11-41 Merritt, 76-41-11—141
47-77 Merry, 65-47-77—774
39-97 Meta, 3545-39—949
71-17 Metcalf, 27-38-59—355
31-81 Mibo, 54-75-31—135
01-46 Micah, 2-2646—462
39-57 Miceto, 17-64-39—946
21-28 Michael, 4-11-28—244
78-84 Michaels, 14-53-58—742
56-88 Mickey, 44-56-74—579
25-50 Middleton, 25-36-65—318
26-62 Midell, 74-62-26—627
12-44 Midian, 1-34 63—364
20-96 Miguel, 25-53-73—532
40-36 Mijarez, 9-43-57—704
48-59 Milan, 32-34-38—346
63-22 Mildred, 3-22-44—424
28-79 Miles, 16-28-35—582
72-87 Milford, 16-24-47—783
06-66 Milicent, 33-40-66—060
23-63 Millard, 62-23-13—123
46-78 Miller, 46-65-68—114
13-41 Millicent, 7-24-60—647
21-59 Milliner, 52-72-59—923
53-65 Mills, 53-65-78—377
95-57 Milo, 38-72-57—222

41-49 Milos, 18-36-41—318
10-60 Milton, 3-10-49—766
34-80 Mimie, 15-61-34—316
34-14 Mims, 32-42-14—428
87-22 Mina, 23-71-28—271
16-30 Mindon, 16-9-30—311
17-47 Minerva, 7-17-47—423
34-57 Ming, 44-57-17—177
57-82 Minietta, 23-73-74—154
31-60 Minion, 19-31-60—114
01-99 Minnette, 13-26-41—146
11-64 Minnie, 5-11-58—652
29-43 Minor, 62-43-31—910
48-56 Minoso, 8-32-38—433
22-98 Minter, 16-55-61—516
30-88 Mintha, 4-28-39—428
03-39 Mintie, 3-10-39—670
15-94 Minton, 19-30-77—774
36-50 Minyard, 69-72-43—431
53-35 Mira, 56-53-35—555
04-73 Miranda, 44-76-64—476
24-10 Miriam, 5-15-24—155
80-72 Mirilla, 29-72-43—897
12-54 Miro, 12-30-54—450
18-48 Missie, 5-18-43—171
10-14 Missouri, 10-14-38—710
83-97 Mister, 25-36-47—345
51-52 Mitchell, 44-52-61—765
14-62 Mittie, 30-57-62—657
68-77 Mobile, 68-46-77—333
28-44 Mobley, 14-36-44—113
40-60 Modesto, 20-40-60-4)00
14-23 Modora, 6-17-31—136
30-66 Moffitt, 30-59-78—433
09-90 Mohamed, 45-50-62—254
36-65 Mohawk, 36-45-65-433
44-74 Mojeeda, 58-77-44—758
58-85 Molise, 70-58-61—586
19-29 Molina, 13-29-50—438
56-71 Mollie, 56-3-71—072
37-83 Molly, 27-37-48—432
13-37 Moms, 18-32-52—238
45-90 Mona, 7-46-45—467
53-61 Monica, 53-55-58—003
23-52 Monie, 59-78-23—278
47-58 Monino, 33-71-47—423
44-65 Monroe, 8-44-65—712
23-75 Mont, 7-32-54—312

67-78 Montague, 50-56-78—110
26-91 Montalvo, 34-47-26—276
14-08 Monte, 8-19-60—902
59-95 Montell, 69-27-48—678
32-96 Monteros, 7-11-9—843
75-84 Monterrey, 42-46-75—510
02-27 Montgomery, 39-49-5—671
76-68 Montoro, 19-35-20—332
31-46 Monty, 7-31-38—312
19-59 Monzella, 19-59-57—330
31-39 Moon, 8-65-9—119
68-75 Moore, 68-75-38—077
46-87 Moran, 46-59-8—119
100-3 Moratin, 20-35-48—335
31-65 More, 43-54-65—401
74-57 Morehead, 56-74-48—988
05-42 Morel, 32-35-65—356
36-89 Moreno, 14-42-36—624
23-54 Morgan, 23-45-54—997
51-95 Morman, 27-68-51—185
11-81 Morrell, 3-53-75—335
30-40 Morrie, 30-40-59—488
63-16 Morris, 33-22-71—614
38-74 Morrison, 38-48-74—455
36-38 Mortimer, 13-26-36—7366
13-87 Mortin, 13-45-54—322
41-29 Morton, 34-56-78—887
36-63 Mosby, 14-36-54—976
49-59 Moses, 37-49-59—098
55-25 Mosley, 38-64-66—556
18-32 Moss, 18-32-54—443
27-72 Mossaic, 31-29-62—557
14-18 Motley, 14-36-18—413
49-62 Motts, 33-16-54—432
30-48 Mount, 30-48-8—893
17-71 Mourita, 12-16-55—070
29-34 Mozart, 12-11-77—171
11-56 Mozell, 8-11-56—410
24-79 Mozella, 2-64-24—262
49-93 Mozelle, 31-56-76—567
18-86 Munalon, 25-40-18—104
33-45 Mundy, 3-7-45—351
28-63 Mungo, 39-52-63—378
03-71 Munoz, 12-24-71—124
38-54 Munsey, 42-10-37—370
04-44 Muriel, 1-4-44—009
14-33 Murphy, 2-10-33—760
19-48 Murray, 8-12-69—432

11-78 Murry, 6-46-38—400
7-100 Music, 23-74-64—423
61-70 Mutt, 1-63-70—070
14-44 Muzza, 3-14-44—867
39-56 Myles, 51-67-39—961
06-70 Myra, 11-70-6—716
26-46 Myram, 38-73-46—373
10-20 Myriam, 62-66-72—266
41-81 Myrick, 20-41-53—351
38-53 Myrilla, 9-38-53—538
53-92 Myrna, 2-53-24—824
47-77 Myron, 50-65-77—791
33-85 Myrtice, 22-8-33—382
27-69 Myrtis, 37-61-27—213
66-72 Myrtle, 29-44-72—804

# N

03-31 Nada, 3-31-53—353
12-24 Nadine, 25-39-74—321
30-60 Nails, 10-36-60—661
07-21 Naldo, 21-49-7—798
34-52 Nance, 34-45-52—007
57-75 Nancey, 6-7-14—374
19-27 Nancy, 8-19-27—680
99-39 Nanette, 7-12-39—622
50-67 Nanine, 12-41-59—533
41-63 Nannie, 41-63-44—268
03-13 Naomi, 2-3-13—329
22-37 Napoleon, 1-41-37—743
37-73 Napolian, 37-73-35—332
01-33 Napp, 24-53-64—782
90-24 Narciso, 5-15-27—155
43-58 Narcisse, 43-58-78—112
14-43 Narcissus, 7-14-69—439
49-67 Narris, 37-67-48—876
34-42 Narvaez, 54-64-34—465
22-78 Nash, 15-22-38—377
07-59 Nashum, 26-45-59—954
14-73 Nat, 14-37-55—103
57-89 Natala, 72-57-47—757
61-67 Natalie, 27-67-53—401
48-98 Natalio, 65-6-48—866
16-57 Nathan, 9-31-52—352
24-32 Nathalael, 4-24-32—214
12-88 Nathaniel, 12-67-78—278
38-42 Nattie, 24-73-42—473
65-81 Navarra, 13-25-36—356
22-35 Navarrete, 46-56-22—205

16-19 Naylor, 11-16-19—333
62-37 Neal, 56-29-37—016
97-47 Neally, 2-12-14—311
34-56 Ned, 34-56-49—080
64-76 Nedra, 9-34-76—967
13-36 Neftali, 3-13-36-414
59-73 Neighbors, 9-16-73—931
44-71 Neil, 13-73-43—731
34-55 Neisner, 34-55-58—832
06-66 Nelida, 12-24-66-664
15-96 Nell, 35-47-15—143
21-29 Nellie, 33-61-29—467
30-36 Nelly, 32-55-5—443
07-17 Nelson, 7-17-69—917
51-63 Nemesia, 11-57-63—301
82-45 Nena, 23-38-66—006
10-17 Neola, 10-17-69—518
63-84 Nepomuceno, 3-78-6—378
11-77 Nesbitt, 44-11-77—005
23-83 Neson, 36-43-49—492
11-78 Nester, 1-11-78—110
47-74 Nestor, 48-76-37—332
02-21 Netcher, 2-21-58—278
32-39 Nettie, 5-32-67—923
10-19 Nettles, 53-58-77—711
26-65 Netty, 70-65-43—455
73-37 Neva, 12-31-45—432
30-56 Nevada, 30-40-56—322
84-56 Neville, 34-54-68—001
29-62 Newberry, 43-53-78—113
08-80 Newby, 14-31-40—001
43-50 Newcombe, 13-43-50—339
91-70 Newell, 31-42-70—007
38-79 Newsby, 34-8-38—993
51-25 Newton, 26-14-49—411
12-32 Neysmith, 13-32-53—003
17-34 Nicasio, 6-28-44—428
02-43 Niceto, 16-53-73—335
09-11 Nicey, 9-11-19—543
48-58 Nicholas, 52-50-59—590
52-66 Nichols, 17-43-52—231
32-43 Nick, 32-43-54—433
13-72 Nickerson, 1-18-71—118
12-21 Nicola, 7-12-69—287
21-40 Nicholas, 21-40-71—068
21-11 Nicolette, 2-5-11—357
23-92 Nigel, 29-63-70—073
09-41 Niles, 35-74-78—341

27-36 Nina, 12-14-36—170
07-17 Ninette, 7-17-54—544
03-77 Nix, 7-42-52—224
53-36 Nixon, 36-77-78—345
19-39 Noah, 8-19-62—991
42-57 Nobilus, 34-57-72—277
45-51 Noble, 23-45-51—551
93-18 Nocola, 62-70-18—027
11-76 Noel, 19-30-51—139
26-40 Nokomis, 9-10-29—713
10-54 Nola, 61-74-54—746
31-81 Nolan, 8-31-61—113
35-68 Nolton, 35-48-78—324
50-60 Noma, 17-19-38—331
35-94 Nona, 41-69-35—394
04-64 Nooley, 20-32-64—623
75-82 Nora, 50-60-75—050
08-11 Norah, 4-8-11—212
23-27 Norene, 68-27-23—269
59-95 Norfolk, 37-56-68—003
21-39 Norine, 33-49-11—148
35-55 Norfleet, 2-40-59—902
30-87 Noriser, 9-21-14—142
27-50 Norma, 14-56-27—333
14-05 Norman, 48-35-50—505
29-73 Norment, 5-12-73—372
28-42 Norris, 13-43-56—544
35-53 North, 35-47-53—453
36-86 Norton, 75-36-6—366
45-56 Norvell, 45-31-56—118
61-77 Norwood, 17-35-77—773
61-69 Novack, 8-43-54—551
55-75 Novella, 24-55-67—454
9-100 Nowell, 39-67-76—639
20-30 Nuby, 22-34-30-034
85-38 Nuflo, 10-58-38—851
46-70 Numa, 48-77-70—777
67-16 Nunez, 8-16-24—426
85-53 Nuno, 3-26-37—763
09-40 Nydia, 47-59-68—523
35-76 Nyles, 35-33-76—335
27-43 Nylon, 13-43-54—990

# O

31-45 Oakes, 31-45-78—782
11-01 Oates, 6-11-39—350
91-66 Oatman, 25-39-56—776
52-15 Oats, 36-46-52-463

76-78 Obabiah, 43-56-78—003
11-66 Obbie, 6-11-66—762
15-39 Obediah, 1-2-15—125
08-65 Oberlin, 5-6-56—652
13-26 Obren, 6-13-37—357
11-17 O'Brien, 11-17-35—345
93-39 Ocampo, 1-12-39—755
03-09 Ocie, 8-18-28—888
14-51 Octavia, 59-67-42—063
67-78 Octavio, 45-67-78—963
18-58 Octavius, 58-53-18—881
38-19 Odas, 12-19-27—070
3-100 O'Day, 32-43-56—119
24-64 Odell, 24-31-67—660
14-69 Odena, 14-11-69—410
35-75 Odessa, 71-35-78—537
25-35 Odesser, 35-76-59 -911
25-35 Odessia, 25-35-45—305
32-59 Odie, 45-32-71—664
53-73 Odis, 53-46-73—013
53-92 Odom, 5-53-74-456
37-81 Ogden, 17-36-45—421
18-81 Oglesby, 18-33-59—590
100-9 O'Hare, 11-77-66—776
15-33 Ola, 15-21-33—625
10-63 Olainae, 3-10-71—071
49-93 Olden, 19-37-56—765
36-74 Oldham, 76-74-36-413
10-39 O'Leary, 10-39-54—450
24-84 Olegario, 57-67-24—675
07-12 Olga, 4-24-34—244
21-36 Olin, 26-36-76—672
65-43 Olivares, 43-54-65—871
94-65 Olive, 65-39-28—240
65-69 Oliver, 3-18-69—465
62-71 Olivet, 4-16-71—919
31-48 Olivia, 12-21-42—438
35-59 Ollie, 5-9-45—551
30-49 Olson, 30-49-65—864
23-95 Olympe, 44-66-23—213
26-06 Olympia, 38-51-66—876
08-83 Omar, 8-32-56—213
45-05 Omie, 5-32-54—696
17-35 Oneal, 17-35-42—193
73-17 O'Neil, 17-30-67—651
61-34 Oneita, 33-43-34—343
11-22 Onie, 10-23-56—012
17-74 Onis, 22-38-74—748

54-68 Onnie, 7-27-48—778
28-82 Onofre, 13-60-28—063
14-59 Opal, 9-14-59—197
41-62 Ophelia, 54-45-62—781
30-77 Ophilia, 21-30-40—032
04-42 Ora, 4-10-42—523
55-90 Ora Lee, 49-73-55—374
55-99 Oralia, 61-72-55—726
04-44 Oreda, 4-19-44—688
21-48 Oregon, 2-16-48—358
42-66 Orelia, 78-42-66—266
29-89 Orestes, 12-20-28—801
39-89 Oreta, 69-39-28—893
02-22 Oretha, 39-50-60—005
38-78 Oriana, 2-22-38—222
18-69 Oribel, 19-62-69—689
10-56 Oriel, 29-51-56—518
100-2 Orlander, 6-14-2—234
15-43 Orlando, 15-19-7—117
60-88 Orlena, 71-60-24—460
30-98 Orlene, 1-8-40—018
56-91 Orozco, 63-56-41—145
24-68 Orrie, 34-54-68—003
48-84 Orson, 14-48-52—235
32-79 Ortiz, 18-30-52—286
44-70 Orville, 5-23-65—721
26-46 Osborne, 7-17-46—870
14-19 Osburn, 15-64-19—464
78-31 Oscar, 8-78-53—090
37-59 Oshie, 37-44-55—110
57-97 Osmund, 53-74-57—545
03-45 Osorio, 31-41-45—123
63-87 Ossie, 7-10-67—001
13-39 Ossole, 13-39-72—131
27-80 Oswald, 27-38-49—688
08-11 Otero, 8-11-54—453
20-32 Otha, 5-52-36—710
58-76 Othello, 4-59-76—611
69-14 Otis, 29-69-59—77C
43-53 Ott, 43-54-53—880
71-82 Ottie, 54-71-62—673
81-31 Otto, 12-10-31—341
21-59 Overman, 76-45-63—356
04-45 Overton, 12-32-38—331
60-86 Ovida, 11-39-60—370
46-33 Ovieco, 36-45-67—932
12-22 Owen, 5-22-39—942
22-36 Owens, 14-36-49—981

72-96 Oyarzabal, 5-9-16—956
11-60 Oz, 70-60-10—000
47-82 Ozell, 55-65-68—834
26-11 Ozella, 17-32-42—257
05-16 Ozenia, 75-16-25—536
12-21 Ozie, 12-21-40—444
20-94 Ozzie, 14-63-72—273

# P

43-63 Pablo, 6-27-63—336
31-84 Pachecos, 40-51-31—110
35-73 Padre, 35-16-49—325
26-37 Paes, 2-28-37—337
54-56 Page, 54-56-76—246
15-36 Paine, 18-36-73—348
81-93 Painter, 17-19-36—318
08-19 Pairlee, 28-37-43—373
83-63 Palencia, 13-26-63—662
30-62 Palestine, 5-39-50—905
33-36 Palm, 33-16-36—335
53-61 Palma, 64-53-61—677
37-54 Palmer, 11-33-54—331
18-72 Palmere, 10-18-72—180
42-53 Palms, 62-77-42—247
01-11 Palune, 25-33-11—133
92-96 Palema, 38-29-69—996
07-77 Pamella, 4-12-77—124
61-29 Pancha, 49-76-61—167
34-71 Pancho, 56-34-25—345
44-63 Pandora, 11-14-44 • 444
12-52 Panek, 24-12-52—238
67-82 Panella, 37-67-58—579
39-91 Panfilo, 72-39-46—392
15-18 Pansy, 18-15-40—408
14-41 Papa, 75-41-14—414
33-16 Paralee, 16-59-72—413
70-78 Pardo, 23-61-70—268
17-34 Parelie, 3-48-34—398
28-81 Parilee, 11-36-28—368
47-74 Parkam, 34-37-74—460
51-60 Parker, 25-30-48—276
27-38 Parkham, 27-38-48—348
15-53 Parks, 15-53-57—983
15-35 Parnell, 15-35-65—331
40-90 Parr, 6-32-45—345
44-56 Parrie, 13-44-68—111
21-38 Parrish, 5-11-38—374
78-85 Parson, 43-54-78—312

30-40 Parsons, 10-30-40—000
06-60 Parte, 65-60-6—665
55-62 Parthenia, 21-62-55—718
29-16 Pasqual, 47-73-29—937
37-46 Pasquini, 10-35-46—852
69-80 Pastor, 2-22-69—974
12-37 Pat, 2-12-35—963
59-66 Patience, 9-11-66—101
20-50 Paton, 14-35-63—341
03-11 Patricia, 3-11-56—528
11-32 Patricio, 8-11-32—254
65-89 Patrick, 28-71-74—287
15-39 Patriece, 9-11-66—101
05-68 Patsy, 6-14-32—214
32-78 Patterson, 32-54-78—345
53-74 Pattie, 28-71-74—718
08-16 Patton, 8-16-72—268
29-69 Paul, 59-69-74—580
32-95 Paula, 32-35-57—874
39-09 Pauletta, 29-52-39—527
02-22 Paulette, 7-15-22—234
44-66 Paulina, 41-44-22—441
09-19 Pauline, 9-19-71—096
21-38 Paulino, 53-38-21—835
64-96 Paulita, 16-64-68—667
47-54 Paxton, 23-43-54—341
21-33 Payo, 70-33-21—102
75-85 Payne, 15-36-38—136
43-65 Payton, 43-54-65—997
34-55 Paz, 54-69-58—896
10-34 Peaches, 17-30-34—437
22-56 Peachy, 42-56-62—566
37-67 Peaks, 39-67-55—098
76-97 Pearce, 16-28-39—982
45-51 Pearl, 45-27-51—657
29-52 Pearlee, 68-52-29—897
09-11 Pearlette, 9-11-78—001
35-75 Pearlie, 30-35-75—575
11-56 Pearline, 18-31-56—681
67-78 Pearlman, 32-48-78—332
28-18 Pearson, 28-40-18—842
14-07 Peck, 7-14-65—560
23-65 Pedradas, 55-65-70—567
28-66 Pedro, 5-11-66—201
36-77 Pegas, 43-77-36—674
46-59 Peggy, 1-32-66—542
100-1 Peggye, 1-32-66—542
41-10 Pelagio, 32-56-10—016

98-80 Pelayo, 78-62-36—679
12-86 Peleg, 8-19-12—123
51-62 Pelina, 67-57-47—747
24-66 Pelt, 44-24-33—342
35-76 Pena, 35-36-76—314
03-47 Pendelton, 4-12-43—441
40-78 Pendrel, 57-78-40—785
19-27 Penelope, 2-19-27—597
30-32 Penister, 8-30-32—320
58-67 Pennie, 33-26-56—662
25-99 Penns, 1-20-25—201
13-27 Penny, 3-13-37—733
27-87 Penson, 45-58-72—284
39-48 Peola, 66-48-39—976
42-79 People, 42-56-70-432
04-26 Peoples, 74-26-4—446
38-67 Pepe, 46-59-67—951
10-33 Pepita, 10-33-47—433
32-38 Peppers, 14-32-61—775
14-49 Peppo, 21-34-14—442
26-66 Percival, 34-51-66—329
27-88 Percora, 9-60-27—987
95-66 Percy, 13-43-53—344
56-75 Perdigoes, 4-42-4—652
28-49 Perdita, 17-25-49—257
03-85 Perdock, 10-74-3—301
52-67 . Perdure, 35-55-52—253
43-53 Peregrine, 7-43-53—743
21-35 Peres, 12-21-35—522
12-60 Pereyra, 65-60-12—066
35-74 Perez, 35-71-72—372
14-37 Peri, 5-16-37—715
07-77 Perina, 7-10-77—007
94-56 Perkins, 31 -53-56—911
56-66 Perry, 56-66-68—380
56-58 Perryman, 31-45-58—762
66-84 Person, 21-39-54—187
20-42 Pessanhas, 43-20-42—204
36-76 Pete, 3-36-76—113
22-45 Peter, 9-20-73—973
34-58 Peters, 5-34-58—561
67-90 Petersen, 43-54-78—651
13-46 Peterson, 13-35-46—742
36-93 Pettibone, 50-31-74—871
19-73 Pettigrew, 5-33-38—873
07-21 Pettrie, 7-11-21—111
41-46 Pettry, 18-27-46—479
83-99 Petty, 36-44-38—833

34-56 Pharoah, 7-34-78—990
61-92 Phears, 56-61-42—201
08-25 Phebie, 12-66-25—576
68-82 Phelix, 28-68-72—298
13-62 Phelps, 13-57-62—762
39-51 Pheobe, 75-51-39—915
26-56 Pheobie, 19-26-56—266
49-10 Phil, 45-10-49—908
30-37 Philbert, 5-28-37—376
02-56 Philemon, 14-63-70—703
21-32 Philip, 21-40-50—005
26-98 Phillie, 37-57-26—667
19-45 Phillip, 5-19-45—112
69-91 Phillipa, 46-67-69—987
37-40 Phillippa, 3-9-40—409
40-44 Phillips, 42-44-73—744
35-55 Phillis, 5-12-38—508
09-29 Philomena, 9-29-47—664
27-36 Phineas, 27-32-59—225
38-62 Phoebe, 8-21-42 018
40-70 Phyllis, 6-9-13—31⸱
11-77 Pickett, 1-11-77—177
62-73 Pickford, 9-68-73—973
30-80 Piedad, 29-58-34—385
14-17 Pierce, 7-13-20—236
05-48 Pierre, 68-76-48—847
35-46 Pierson, 35-46-39—110
32-68 Pilar, 32-50-68—680
22-30 Pillows, 3-30-31—311
13-54 Pinchie, 26-54-73—457
40-54 Pinckney, 2-13-54—544
35-67 Pineda, 8-35-67—447
43-76 Pinkie, 41-64-76—646
36-27 Pinky, 11-16-36—116
34-46 Pio, 34-53-46—354
21-65 Pitman, 6-24-65—245
49-74 Pittman, 49-30-74—438
68-86 Pitts, 48-39-1—481
08-96 Pius, 63-66-8—666
14-39 Placido, 14-39-48—622
43-63 Pleasant, 78-63-53—876
59-77 Plutarco, 72-77-59—978
01-11 Plymouth, 40-52-11—123
33-27 Poe, 6-28-45—452
28-74 Pogue, 28-63-74—674
11-26 Poinciano, 2-23-11—143
31-36 Pointer, 34-36-53—113
19-37 Pola, 19-37-52—423

89-97 Pole, 33-62-9—623
35-53 Policarpo, 3-15-51—515
39-78 Polk, 33-39-74—473
23-58 Pollard, 23-40-76—237
40-87 Pollie, 20-30-40—002
06-66 Polly, 6-12-66—722
38-51 Polo, 61-71-51—115
14-44 Pomona, 9-32-50—589
11-22 Pompilio, 1-22-39—937
18-72 Poncho, 78-72-18—184
12-14 Ponder, 8-14-37—761
29-46 Ponnie, 49-46-29—923
46-64 Poole, 8-25-56—560
06-32 Pooler, 70-32-6—621
11-42 Pope, 11-42-63—356
29-79 Popolo, 23-44-29—449
15-57 Poppy, 9-46-72—946
30-40 Porcel, 48-60-33—064
88-50 Porfirio, 31-38-50—508
59-69 Porter, 59-59-69—099
49-47 Porterfield, 49-52-7—752
31-61 Portia, 27-31-61—613
4-100 Portland, 29-35-45—542
03-05 Portocarrerc, 1-3-50—505
13-63 Potts, 13-57-63—653
23-71 Poue, 23-34-55—534
44-54 Powe, 14-44-54—444
72-27 Powell, 16-27-62—762
38-89 Powers, 38-47-63—653
76-81 Pozo, 30-47-76—347
04-39 Prado, 21-39-4—934
16-63 Prathro, 8-69-16—946
49-78 Pratts, 12-53-78—788
31-24 Praxedes, 59-24-31—114
09-90 Preacly, 77-9-29—993
12-39 Precious, 12-11-39—212
47-97 Prentice, 12-43-56—444
32-78 Presbyter, 7-32-78—661
08-18 Prescott, 8-11-18—360
24-40 Presley, 24-40-60-426
19-27 Preston, 56-78-51—767
59-38 Prewitt, 7-32-38—661
34-49 Price, 11-18-54—511
07-14 Priester, 7-14-65—466
13-39 Primalia, 1-13-39—139
42-53 Primas, 6-10-66—880
11-44 Primavera, 11-44-18—184
24-48 Primo, 24-48-6—648

18-26 Primrose, 3-7-11—311
38-54 Prince, 24-38-54—015
31-38 Princeas, 19-31-78—198
31-38 Princess, 32-48-74—977
68-72 Princeton, 32-3448—412
51-11 Prior, 11-27-51—171
82-93 Priscella, 16-29-58—978
26-64 Priscilla, 4-24-54—651
39-54 Pritchard, 16-56-78—568
62-90 Pritchett, 21-30-55—503
33-54 Proctor, 54-33-52—760
27-41 Prolis, 17-2741—188
86-17 Prospero, 11-17-77—771
51-76 Prudence, 51-76-32—661
06-47 Prudencio, 30-31-70—370
18-48 Pruitt, 8-18-48—018
14-25 Prunella, 10-16-57—476
07-11 Pryor, 7-11-36—237
26-33 Puckett, 43-65-49—776
38-42 Pueblo, 16-3842—255
92-31 Pugh, 28-30-31—342
83-57 Pullen, 43-44-57—577
12-77 Pullins, 12-36-77—217
19-31 Pullman, 19-31-6—190
12-21 Pulman, 12-21-75—215
73-38 Pumphrey, 32-34-38—348
69-76 Purdue, 1345-74—401
20-40 Purdy, 20-39-58—388
98-73 Purificación, 7-25-3—453
30-64 Purnell, 30-36-64—364
48-59 Pusey, 47-48-59—455
01-65 Putman, 7-14-53—453
65-56 Putnam, 44-39-56—114
11-54 Pye, 11-54-57—571

# Q

40-60 Quack, 345-56—544
31-46 Quaile, 31-38-52—352
20-63 Quaker, 16-20-63—163
57-32 Quality, 38-43-71—713
19-29 Qualls, 5-19-29—519
77-16 Quaresmas, 42-72-8—724
34-53 Quarles, 16-34-53—530
39-42 Quarrie, 5-9-42—592
42-64 Quarry, 6-22-64—622
12-28 Quay, 12-28-43—004
20-73 Quayle, 43-62-73—473
06-16 Quedellis, 6-16-49—011

12-59 Queen, 22-42-59—259
05-28 Queener, 5-15-28—932
18-48 Queenie, 8-18-48—582
08-18 Queenster, 8-18-48—482
23-37 Quentin, 23-37-40—402
46-48 Quentina, 46-48-76—476
91-77 Quento, 28-65-77—270
35-50 Querry, 7-28-75—275
21-77 Quesada, 21-37-77—772
43-81 Quick, 29-55-65—487
04-54 Quigley, 37-48-67—367
18-28 Quin, 22-28-42—429
52-61 Quincy, 52-61-39—563
75-85 Quinlan, 28-37-58—536
18-36 Quinn, 18-36-74—184
36-63 Quinnie, 25-37-64—432
29-71 Quinones, 29-39-71—192
37-67 Quinten, 7-37-67—767
89-52 Quintero, 15-52-55—555
94-67 Quintina, 26-37-67—673
07-17 Quinton, 7-17-37—101
36-80 Quintus, 36-15-&—853
03-13 Quitman, 45-18-32—552

# R

99-60 Rachael, 3-58-60—560
20-22 Rachel, 2-20-22—123
95-69 Rachelle, 57-60-69—690
44-88 Radcliffe, 77-58-7—753
74-38 Raden, 25-38-67—657
34-62 Rader, 26-34-51—251
22-84 Radford, 2-52-58—268
30-51 Rae, 20-30-51—100
09-55 Rafael, 46-73-77—467
32-52 Rafferty, 32-52-69—359
02-79 Ragan, 32-60-17—377
46-70 Raglan, 46-52-17—348
14-66 Ragland, 20-32-45—324
17-40 Raglin, 4-17-40—400
15-58 Raimundo, 15-58-61.—161
27-37 Raines, 58-61-75—116
11-66 Rainey, 7-11-66—166
23-87 Raleigh, 32-48-67—300
20-46 Ralph, 20-46-66—438
61-63 Ralston, 51-63-68—568
78-52 Ramirez, 14-52-78—524
15-45 Ramiro, 15-30-45—305
10-38 Ramon, 5-10-38—897

24-31 Ramona, 24-29-31—142
34-37 Ramsey, 3-34-37—345
56-75 Ramos, 15-26-75—156
18-61 Rand, 17-18-61—671
08-38 Randall, 8-11-38—811
96-61 Randolph, 12-35-61—132
14-52 Ranier, 14-52-8—588
08-14 Rannie, 14-51-72-412
39-61 Ranny, 29-39-61—193
52-57 Ransom, 39-48-57—375
69-19 Raoul, 8-19-39—998
47-93 Raphael, 22-47-39—724
17-99 Rapley, 68-17-62—622
10-72 Rapozos, 10-30-72—301
60-51 Rapp, 8-18-51—181
33-42 Rascus, 42-33-14—344
27-86 Rashell, 17-27-46—776
67-73 Rastus, 26-67-73—367
05-55 Raul, 67-72-75—672
18-46 Raven, 21-19-18—891
34-51 Rawls, 34-51-73—341
40-65 Ray, 38-27-65—070
10-76 Raybum, 2-10-76—381
51-67 Rayfield, 51-78-67—766
18-61 Rayford, 18-26-61—361
05-55 Raymond, 5-11-55—888
12-20 Rayster, 12-20-69—210
33-94 Reaka, 16-29-33—961
68-80 Real, 42-38-68—838
59-73 Reatha, 35-59-73—953
28-57 Reaves, 28-51-57—251
26-45 Reba, 5-10-58—510
11-65 Rebecca, 5-11-65—621
14-17 Rebekah, 14-17-67—114
88-67 Rector, 45-67-59—469
51-85 Red, 21-51-61—006
18-47 Redd, 18-25-47—418
100-9 Reddick, 53-62-9—903
09-32 Redding, 19-9-28—299
29-58 Redman, 15-36-70—635
56-77 Redmond, 1-56-77—156
48-74 Ree, 19-48-38—884
08-68 Reece, 8-10-68—606
60-70 Reed, 33-60-70—390
04-45 Reenie, 274-45-447
67-86 Reeny, 26-67-76—776
28-35 Reeves, 28-32-35—253
29-36 Reggie, 3942-57—678

49-95 Regina. 36-16-21—112
62-83 Reginald, 12-10-11—301
33-66 Reid, 33-36-66—366
16-32 Reina, 21-37-48—847
24-42 Rejoiner, 1-22-42—242
75-89 Remigio, 11-18-32—811
26-44 Remijio, 26-44-16—164
38-75 Remington, 38-47-75—658
48-63 Remires, 26-48-63—378
15-31 Remirez, 7-12-19—927
03-38 Remo, 33-3-38—333
18-56 Rena, 6-18-56—945
66-50 Render, 25-50-66—650
06-92 Rene, 17-31-66—113
34-70 Renee, 25-37-70—707
63-77 Renfrow, 63-68-77—678
20-70 Renita, 6-30-70—367
28-87 Reola, 10-16-28—146
11-71 Rera, 11-31-71—131
40-48 Ressye, 21-40-48—408
53-81 Restrepo, 4-24-53—534
62-72 Retta, 36-62-72—627
64-76 Reuben, 18-64-76—186
79-98 Reva, 15-48-59—948
11-19 Revall, 7-11-19—222
6-100 Revell, 56-68-51—561
70-75 Revels, 20-29-70—992
07-67 Reven, 7-17-67—177
38-78 Revie, 9-35-38—353
21-91 Rex, 21-41-52—251
63-76 Rey, 21-63-76—663
01-31 Reyes, 24-28-31—184
41-97 Reynaldo, 3-31-41—113
29-82 Reynold, 14-22-29—292
63-77 Reynolds, 1-63-77—163
32-56 Rhoads, 5-32-56—110
07-77 Rhoda, 7-10-77—582
35-54 Rhodes, 4-11-56—411
12-24 Ribandeira, 5-12-24—245
35-76 Ricardo, 12-35-76—455
11-23 Ricart, 2-11-23—211
35-58 Rice, 35-52-58—350
22-77 Rich, 1-51-68—682
42-66 Richard, 31-66-78—876
14-30 Richards, 14-52-72—122
31-42 Richardson, 4-54-66—561
56-64 Richey, 56-76-78—112
28-39 Richman, 28-39-7-4)04

13-55 Richmond, 4-11-55-411
57-70 Rickie, 57-60-70—567
11-23 Ricky, 11-23-54—123
15-17 Riddle, 17-35-72—175
36-69 Ridge, 18-32-51—419
23-32 Ridgeway, 22-39-50—200
49-78 Ridley, 18-25-78—189
02-96 Riggins, 10-39-58—105
32-77 Riggs, 32-35-77—250
77-66 Riley, 11-35-77—177
65-56 Ring, 1-11-76—108
24-54 Ringer, 24-54-76—108
14-84 Ringling, 4-10-60—417
29-69 Rio, 9-29-69—711
29-76 Riordan, 23-29-76—927
08-37 Rios, 2-37-27—772
23-43 Riperda, 13-23-43—323
44-77 Ripley, 41-44-77—477
68-90 Ripperda, 13-34-68—431
25-57 Risa, 8-20-57—208
93-68 Rita, 17-18-60—187
11-30 Ritter, 11-30-34—344
51-65 Ritz, 16-65-76—755
18-64 Rivas, 15-18-47—450
25-35 Rivera, 36-49-25—943
50-78 Rivero, 50-15-78—554
03-59 Rivers, 3-10-35—366
46-63 Roa, 46-48-63—312
28-54 Roach, 14-54-67—766
46-54 Roao, 35-54-59—330
81-18 Robbie, 7-57-18—188
87-98 Robbin, 26-38-44—384
45-65 Robbs, 45-54-65-451
34-90 Roberson, 68-34-21—419
44-74 Robert, 8-24-49—249
39-62 Roberta, 6-45-62—439
50-86 Robertina, 28-78-50—297
11-66 Robertine, 11-18-66—585
58-63 Roberto, 20-43-63—563
15-20 Roberts, 10-15-48—110
19-43 Robertson, 19-44-51—451
19-99 Robeson, 19-32-42—881
11-33 Robin, 12-50-33—053
21-11 Robins, 33-50-73—350
66-77 Robinson, 1-57-66—677
63-80 Robson, 50-67-78—411
17-73 Roda, 19-29-73—991
24-48 Roderic, 6-21-48—286

77-85 Roderick, 69-77-49—747
47-51 Rodgers, 47-60-51—500
69-89 Rodia, 58-69-22—292
42-55 Rodney, 5-8-55—770
79-83 Rodolfo, 51-60-71—160
04-62 Rodolph, 18-37-62—267
57-72 Rodolphus, 3-57-72—177
61-97 Rodrigo, 44-61-70—643
32-44 Rodrigues,11-9-3 2—291
12-29 Rodríguez, 12-29-34—129
32-45 Roemer, 11-32-45—345
29-36 Rogelio, 72-36-29—356
10-24 Roger, 1-10-24—096
12-33 Rogers, 33-54-60—530
32-63 Roland, 3-46-63—346
70-94 Roldan, 22-70-33—799
10-30 Rolf, 59-70-30—738
41-62 Rolfe, 30-52-62—738
36-15 Rolinda, 15-55-66—127
100-9 Rolins, 17-9-39—910
05-55 Rolland, 5-15-55—555
49-88 Rolle, 45-60-49—456
62-73 Rollie, 2-10-62—198
18-40 Rollins, 18-19-40—311
78-81 Romelia, 28-49-78—784
29-61 Romeo, 29-45-61—373
31-56 Romero, 38-46-56—546
95-16 Romito, 10-23-16—123
23-61 Romola, 5-31-61—568
19-36 Romulo, 27-71-36—717
26-67 Ronald, 14-35-67—624
09-82 Ronaldo, 42-48-9—178
4-100 Roque, 56-67-44—756
12-21 Rosa, 12-21-40—771
45-92 Rosabel, 45-23-7—237
52-98 Rosabelle, 77-52-32—504
26-49 Rosalee, 44-49-36—711
78-87 Rosalie, 2-41-78—687
12-31 Rosalind, 34-55-12—125
33-66 Rosalinde, 26-66-33—636
42-54 Rosaline, 2-10-42—662
08-75 Rosalyn, 8-12-75—578
27-49 Rosamira, 13-76-49—794
83-60 Rosamond, 1-11-60—011
47-96 Rosane, 54-65-74—569
46-62 Rosanna, 40-46-62—244
29-53 Rosanne, 47-53-29—537
02-33 Rosario, 8-25-33—583

Names Names

37-73 Rosco, 64-37-73—337
26-56 Roscoe, 6-9-56—908
18-56 Rose, 7-18-56—185
50-62 Rosebud, 3-12-5 <—007
51-91 Roselyn, 15-51-61—115
62-07 Roseman, 33-62-7—627
28-34 Rosemary, 75-34-28—834
12-18 Rosena, 5-18-47—888
13-84 Rosendo, 24-13-8—113
47-65 Rosero, 63-65-47—500
18-40 Rosetta, 6-18-40—653
04-16 Rosie, 4-16-32—785
21-54 Rosina, 39-53-54—543
38-56 Rosine, 56-48-32—332
01-76 Rosnell, 1-21-76—231
29-62 Ross, 29-37-62—297
29-34 Rossman, 5-30-34—543
07-11 Rosy, 7-11-56-455
59-67 Rota, 7-5-67—757
67-76 Roth, 7-14-76—001
15-41 Rotha, 15-41-60—432
11-77 Rothchild, 11-47-77—117
14-29 Rove, 32-62-29—941
17-32 Rowan, 17-32-50—503
48-52 Rowe, 54-69-52—566
22-39 Rowena, 15-74-39—739
50-55 Rowland, 16-50-76—607
12-14 Roxana, 12-14-56—321
14-34 Roxanna, 34-47-77—477
34-55 Roxanne, 37-55-8—119
19-33 Roxie, 19-30-33—065
60-68 Roy, 8-10-68—776
31-61 Royal, 31-61-72—800
30-71 Rozena, 4-73-30—167
30-71 Rozenna, 4-73-30—167
15-77 Rozina, 61-65-77—756
06-40 Roben, 16-6-40—678
07-20 Rubetta, 11-57-77—517
30-65 Rubiera, 24-30-65—306
21-43 Rubirosa, 33-71-43—731
45-73 Ruby, 8-45-73—529
51-85 Rubye, 56-51-45—555
37-59 Rucker, 8-45-59—923
12-38 Rudder, 12-48-66—665
19-59 Rudolph, 28-59-71—597
56-59 Rudolpho, 55-56-75—755
56-84 Rudolphus, 28-56-77—795
02-32 Rudy, 66-70-32—706

29-79 Ruffin, 20-29-67—229
72-91 Ruffino, 17-34-72—346
91-72 Rufino, 46-72-58—724
28-77 Rufus, 22-38-72—328
33-66 Rui, 77-66-33-637
100-3 Ruiz, 25-33-60—247
36-95 Rumby, 12-36-58—367
13-49 Rupert, 58-49-13—149
44-60 Ruperto, 7-47-60—060
18-28 Rusher, 8-18-28—218
27-52 Rushing, 35-27-52—575
07-11 Russel, 7-11-48-411
21-31 Russell, 21-31-56—001
30-45 Ruth, 45-14-26—190
27-86 Ruthie, 17-27-68—728
01-11 Ruthier, 18-59-11—194
39-67 Ruthy, 76-67-39—977
80-90 Rutland, 6-67-50—607
46-50 Rutlidge, 11-46-50—410
33-45 Ruy, 26-48-33—384
33-50 Ryan, 33-50-69—350
27-57 Ryans, 60-57-27—717

# S

39-92 Saabedra, 2-36-39—936
64-35 Saavedra, 27-2-64—426
53-74 Sabater, 68-53-74-435
61-57 Sabath, 36-57-58—519
23-34 Sabbath, 23-34-37—310
14-17 Sabina, 9-14-17—147
87-96 Sabine, 19-37-61—794
31-44 Sachs, 31-44-74-411
29-69 Sadie, 34-52-69—491
31-35 Sadler, 31-35-66—341
46-97 Saenz, 49-46-12—164
81-66 Sage, 50-54-66—714
13-31 Saint, 13-31-55—551
54-75 Sainz, 38-69-75—597
10-31 Saks, 10-17-43-443
64-65 Salemas, 35-64-65—644
62-56 Sales, 37-56-78—456
09-26 Salida, 49-32-57—111
38-42 Salina, 41-65-42—532
02-11 Saline, 2-11-56—327
12-68 Sallie, 2-12-51-611
12-66 Sally, 2-12-66—583
07-77 Salm, 7-77-67—564
03-84 Salmon, 16-22-3—326

42-73 Salome, 44-55-73—545
20-23 Salon, 4-20-23—233
16-61 Salone, 12-61-16—468
90-21 Salterain, 11-29-62—997
24-64 Salustiano, 24-34-64—345
14-50 Saluzzo, 15-65-78—768
31-78 Salvador, 3143-78—694
58-64 Salvatore, 3-23-54—532
47-71 Salvioni, 72-71-41—114
27-52 Sam, 27-37-52-467
07-17 Sanatha, 7-17-57—823
27-77 Sammy, 20-32-77—302
43-63 Sampson, 21-43-63—113
27-30 Sams, 3-5-30—350
49-57 Samson, 1845-57—857
22-89 Samuel, 10-35-44-445
16-32 Samuels, 21-16-32—811
77-83 San, 53-64-77—045
12-94 Sanches, 10-42-12—214
08-57 Sanchez, 8-38-57—837
60-40 Sancho, 14-30-40—500
32-28 Sandalio, 22-73-32—723
17-30 Sanders, 12-17-30—320
04-70 Sanderson, 11-29-31—312
23-77 Sandia, 41-77-23—732
57-69 Sandra, 27-57-69—971
33-63 Sandy, 3-33-63—662
22-48 Sanson, 29-52-22—152
50-56 Santa, 30-50-56—503
16-36 Santalleen, 8-16-36—182
82-93 Santarelli, 16-6-36—006
11-61 Santiago, 11-21-61—111
46-18 Santleen, 13-26-39—196
44-88 Santos, 13-63-44—435
05-55 Sanz, 21-40-55—246
24-42 Sapp, 51-74-42—147
41-33 Sapphire, 70-41-33—341
63-99 Sara, 44-63-68—638
33-60 Sarah, 33-56-60—089
46-76 Sardinahas, 1-12-6—612
09-69 Sargent, 9-37-44—441
15-30 Sarmiento, 4-28-30—843
47-55 Sarine, 39-47-55—055
21-44 Saron, 23-44-15—113
38-82 Saul, 15-38-75—155
29-40 Saulters, 29-40-67—009
35-43 Saunders, 35-43-66—112
25-98 Savannah, 5-25-55—257

06-39 Saverio, 50-62-39—639
16-34 Savilla, 20-75-34—752
31-43 Saxon, 31-46-43—310
10-44 Saxton, 10-22-44—972
37-77 Sayles, 37-56-77—119
41-46 Scales, 50-46-76—451
15-63 Schafer, 53-64-15—643
80-43 Schultz, 13-43-47—479
32-68 Schuyler, 32-65-68—466
26-71 Scipio, 71-45-29—812
13-32 Scott, 13-32-54—341
96-56 Scotty, 32-49-56—703
73-89 Seals, 46-65-49—875
12-58 Searcy, 12-58-69—118
33-50 Sebastian, 24-31-50—651
14-49 Seeger, 27-49-14—149
08-16 Seeley, 8-16-72—017
37-52 Seferiha, 4-44-52—244
04-42 Segura, 35-42-4—485
100-7 Seibert, 22-44-7—732
26-74 Selectman, 2-26-74—746
13-90 Selena, 54-65-13—136
22-34 Selina, 9-22-34-429
0848 Sellers, 8-28-48—879
27-57 Selma, 9-27-57—052
14-32 Serna, 14-26-32—263
35-55 Senalda, 71-55-35—555
35-97 Senator, 14-35-58—500
41-81 Senior, 14-41-69—914
26-42 Señor, 26-14-42—234
42-21 Señora, 66-42-21—124
21-26 Señorita, 45-33-26—698
59-83 Serafin, 12-43-59—943
25-71 Sereathy, 8-55-71—158
27-47 Serema, 17-27-47—277
03-33 Serena, 3-13-33—333
74-81 Sergio, 14-37-49—496
12-98 Serna, 6-12-33—312
31-65 Serrano, 21-31-65—563
52-77 Seth, 52-26-77—776
04-14 Severiano, 4-14-62—014
37-40 Severina, 40-30-37—337
56-89 Severins, 30-36-56—665
40-82 Severo, 46-40-26—406
57-75 Sewell, 13-57-75—570
37-70 Sexton, 2-37-70—001
15-43 Seymour, 2-15-43—171
26-50 Seyvil, 12-50-41—411

91-46 Sharkey, 67-72-46—472
24-66 Sharon, 56-66-24—654
46-76 Sharpe, 16-35-76—432
23-46 Shaw, 39-23-46—336
11-75 Shealy, 11-17-75—577
62-77 Sheila, 62-77-17—177
02-34 Shelby, 7-47-34—437
99-56 Sheldon, 14-56-67—657
57-83 Shelia, 29-57-39—679
23-39 Shell, 23-37-24—421
30-47 Shelley, 15-73-28—207
47-67 Shelly, 47-37-67—368
28-67 Shelton, 67-53-28—723
12-64 Shepard, 28-63-64—463
12-36 Shephard, 12-36-57—118
06-64 Shepherd, 20-70-6—072
12-29 Sheppard, 43-78-29—298
50-38 Sherley, 29-38-56—521
09-14 Sherman, 8-18-78—900
44-88 Sherry, 52-44-31—146
16-62 Sherwood, 12-34-62—257
05-72 Shin, 62-77-72—270
79-95 Shires, 33-69-53—359
09-65 Shirley, 5-9-65—910
15-27 Shores, 19-42-27—277
09-61 Shoulder, 51-61-70—115
60-87 Shuler, 22-24-51—440
22-94 Sias, 11-26-22—621
53-71 Sibley, 61-53-71—135
19-58 Sibyl, 10-19-58—376
86-90 Sibulla, 32-44-38—834
14-78 Sidney, 2-14-78—505
35-42 Sidra, 76-42-35—245
51-60 Siegried, 5-41-51—145
41-63 Sigmund, 18-49-41—326
12-24 Sigrid, 12-24-58—118
29-92 Sihugo, 67-19-12—972
17-63 Silas, 45-63-72—987
43-93 Siliz, 50-60-43—334
17-70 Siller, 18-31-70—078
25-54 Sillman, 25-38-54—331
9-100 Silonis, 9-29-58—599
55-75 Silrenia, 55-65-75—402
25-85 Silva, 68-75-25—257
36-50 Silvas, 25-40-50—050
11-18 Silverta, 11-18-59—477
45-60 Silvester, 6-45-60—064
23-69 Silvertre, 3-6-69—963

18-59 Silvia, 17-59-38—876
22-38 Simeon, 4-38-71—718
24-45 Simon, 24-27-45—245
68-54 Simmons, 30-54-10—345
11-24 Simms, 11-24-65—508
11-56 Simpson, 3-11-56—982
61-70 Sims, 61-34-70—113
37-77 Sina, 20-30-37—020
01-52 Sinclair, 39-49-26—694
69-28 Sinforo, 58-62-28—268
19-93 Sinforoso, 1-3-44—148
22-66 Singer, 22-64-66—356
37-77 Singleton, 24-37-77—341
29-92 Sip, 10-20-29—279
53-84 Sir, 24-53-62—234
10-76 Siruela, 16-66-76—667
12-24 Sivella, 12-24-61—657
26-55 Sively, 5-9-55—171
31-38 Size, 31-38-48—839
07-29 Skitch, 74-29-7—296
20-58 Slade, 38-48-20—204
24-46 Sledge, 24-39-52—365
02-23 Slettie, 8-51-62—218
11-09 Slim, 33-42-11—104
64-77 Sloan, 22-64-77—357
15-39 Sly, 71-39-15—597
36-91 Small, 36-76-75—300
53-58 Smart, 43-65-78—410
13-69 Smidley, 13-69-54—659
32-85 Smiley, 43-38-49—420
47-69 Smily, 2-61-69—662
30-53 Smith, 30-53-78—319
97-18 Smithie, 5-18-27—368
09-32 Smythe, 9-32-58—509
62-74 Sneads, 41-50-62—605
43-60 Sneed, 60-51-43—312
47-06 Snike, 78-47-6—478
80-60 Snipes, 7-17-60—679
23-37 Snodgrass, 1-37-56—449
45-55 Snowden, 55-45-66—554
85-58 Snyder, 43-58-67—972
100-8 Soares, 32-8-16—168
16-24 Solano, 70-16-24—425
33-92 Soldan, 1-60-33—360
02-23 Soler, 23-40-2—243
46-86 Sólita, 49-47-46—466
21-44 Sol, 21-44-37—311
42-58 Solomon, 40-42-58—018

55-73 Sonia, 32-55-64—556
26-59 Sonnie, 6-16-26—216
63-82 Sonny, 59-69-21—129
10-98 Sophia, 77-10-20—001
10-22 Sophie, 5-10-22—659
11-50 Sophronia, 1-11-50—314
15-81 Sophy, 15-30-46^-537
37-59 South, 43-26-59—909
11-36 Southern, 11-40-36—654
34-70 Spam, 31-48-70—708
25-93 Sparks, 15-39-25—529
54-87 Spears, 22-37-60—607
46-68 Speed, 9-44-68—506
75-57 Speedy, 58-68-75—585
17-40 Speights, 23-40-17—719
22-56 Spencer, 22-56-75—770
48-62 Spiney, 14-48-62—244
68-58 Spires, 29-58-68—340
05-25 Springer, 5-25-38—341
99-29 Spruell, 21-29-63—363
11-16 Squalls, 11-16-38—116
64-82 Square, 67-76-64—866
17-27 Stacey, 17-27-73—332
26-76 Stacker, 30-57-26^73
03-55 Stacks, 14-47-55—597
89-18 Stacy, 21-38-18—184
05-55 Stallcup, 5-11-55—753
55-41 Stallins, 55-63-49—824
05-38 Stallworth, 9-72-38—789
14-22 Stan, 25-52-14—145
52-62 Stanislaus, 43-63-52—635
07-33 Stanley, 7-33-27—906
31-36 Staples, 36-15-40—388
21-57 Stapleton, 21-25-37—214
65-77 Starks, 19-65-77—358
66-96 Steam, 25-38-66—366
01-73 Steck, 21-11-1—141
45-51 Steed, 34-45-51—554
37-54 Steele, 2-37-54—355
07-17 Stella, 7-17-47--552
95-68 Steele, 64-68-18—888
05-40 Stephen, 3-5-40—403
08-37 Stephens, 18-44-8-414
30-84 Stephenson, 53-14-8—548
13-79 Stephinia, 10-73-13—337
21-61 Stephinie, 26-61-21—161
07-17 Sterling, 7-17-59—009
36-56 Stevania, 36-53-59—330

90-75 Steven, 30-38-75—008
10-42 Stevens, 1-10-42—324
30-55 Stevenson, 30-55-56—410
67-44 Steward, 37-8-76—309
16-50 Stewart, 5-16-50—601
38-43 Stiles, 1-3843—433
29-72 Stillman, 3-25-39—001
11-55 Stilman, 8-11-55—237
55-78 Stimson, 3-55-29—511
20-43 Stiner, 27-35-20—025
07-60 Stock, 11-35-54—408
24-36 Stokes, 8-24-77—700
30-49 Stone, 3049-56—450
38-69 Stout, 32-38-69—387
05-55 Street, 1-5-55—440
35-65 Streeter, 654647—577
12-21 Strickland, 14-32-57—577
21-29 Strong, 21-29-60—410
53-28 Strothers, 32-53-68—501
38-43 Stuart, 38-54-43—540
43-65 Stubbs, 4-43-65—119
04-44 Suares, 28-54-44—454
71-94 Suber, 36-45-71—178
33-66 Sudie, 12-19-66—691
49-88 Sue, 65-74-48—748
17-67 Suetta, 17-35-67—554
83-19 Suggs, 55-19-29—553
42-78 Sula, 42-61-59—925
33-54 Summers, 43-54-68—308
77-82 Summerville, 3-6-9—369
35-44 Sunta, 66-75-44—457
11-65 Susan, 13-20-11—133
27-72 Susana, 29-37-27—917
15-57 Susanna, 7-15-57—446
38-47 Susannah, 46-56-38—483
05-57 Susetta, 40-45-57—454
12-27 Susette, 18-47-27—507
05-45 Susie, 5-9-45—935
51-64 Sussian, 39-56-64—654
38-78 Sussie, 61-72-38—781
31-45 Susy, 7-31-45—119
22-72 Sutton, 22-39-54—990
57-84 Suzanna, 67-78-57—677
62-46 Suzan, 24-34-46—446
10-97 Suzetta, 55-10-20—002
30-40 Suzette, 6-13-30—013
17-92 Suzie, 46-17-66—674
47-62 Suzy, 73-62-47—628

11-60 Swain, 11-4-60—533
36-74 Swan, 35-36-74—349
100-2 Swanson, 68-54-43—400
10-17 Sweet, 4-10-17—112
7-100 Swift, 38-62-7—679
65-89 Sybel, 12-65-68—942
03-33 Sybil, 26-49-33—946
58-85 Sylva, 8-19-58—973
11-98 Sylvan, 45-68-11—146
34-71 Sylvana, 35-74-34—739
07-11 Sylvester, 7-11-56—320
07-14 Sylvia, 7-14-57—429
16-76 Sylvina, 16-58-76—757
07-14 Symphorosa, 7-14-65—176
26-56 Sypes, 4-11-56—511

# T

28-85 Tadeo, 10-15-43—487
10-15 Taft, 4-10-15—542
24-34 Talbert, 5-11-34—432
11-17 Talbot, 7-11-17—615
23-99 Tallulah, 23-43-54—332
47-39 Talma, 1-10-39—762
15-55 Tamar, 15-37-55—310
36-54 Tamara, 31-36-54—356
41-76 Tamplin, 30-54-76—367
02-66 Taplin, 31-54-78—780
73-57 Tarbert, 1-23-57—193
35-52 Tarson, 13-43-54—600
32-93 Tassie, 6-54-32—768
11-21 Tate, 11-21-66—654
38-50 Tatem, 8-38-63—583
59-79 Taveiras, 11-45-6—585
43-54 Taylor, 21-43-54—409
67-73 Teal, 2-37-28—388
04-14 Teddie, 4-14-56—651
38-68 Teena, 28-65-68—266
29-48 Tegan, 20-44-29—459
07-74 Telesforo, 1-11-15—541
24-42 Tellez, 27-51-24—144
36-86 Temistocles, 4-36-26—663
19-56 Temperance, 11-19-5—562
12-68 Temple, 68-54-55—498
10-16 Templeton, 2-10-16—210
16-63 Tenna, 25-66-16—667
07-78 Tennessee, 4-7-73—388
33-56 Tensley, 48-60-33—064
39-71 Teodora, 29-37-71—792

04-91 Teodoro, 14-4-44—549
20-50 Teodula, 41-54-20—024
21-37 Tera, 77-21-37—731
83-26 Terence, 7-23-76—873
09-77 Teresa, 71-9-77—279
17-32 Teressa, 17-65-32—657
15-62 Terrell, 33-15-62—153
55-90 Terrence, 3-39-55—950
56-65 Terry, 15-38-65—502
37-70 Thad, 37-54-76—411
45-82 Thaddeus, 4-19-74—417
39-71 Thalia, 22-26-39—530
26-49 Tharotan, 53-26-49—264
31-74 Thatcher, 31-32-74—420
96-61 Theda, 47-32-61—952
38-47 Thelia, 70-47-53—834
07-27 Thelma, 7-19-27—916
20-89 Theo, 42-20-35—459
14-61 Theobald, 9-32-75—471
34-27 Theoda, 19-27-38—321
76-81 Theodora, 64-76-57—532
22-34 Theodore, 1-22-34—123
69-43 Theodosa, 31-69-43—092
47-67 Theodoshia, 7-47-67—116
36-71 Theola, 6-36-71—713
16-66 Theonita, 15-55-45—555
44-81 Theophil, 45-52-59—459
20-31 Theresa, 58-78-20—253
36-54 Therese, 50-36-54—536
25-45 Theressa, 3-16-45—521
88-95 Theretha, 21-38-40—379
06-66 Therest, 37-52-66—625
57-75 Thereza, 10-63-57—361
19-49 Thersa, 30-43-69—976
05-12 Thomas, 5-12-78—517
05-12 Thomasa, 5-12-78—512
35-43 Thomasena, 5-15-35—123
25-56 Thomasetta, 2-25-56—855
30-43 Thomasina, 7-30-43—307
13-87 Thomasine, 37-13-7—136
27-77 Thompson, 40-77-78—708
60-80 Thomson, 21-43-56—445
13-54 Thora, 2-13-54—211
53-65 Thorndale, 11-42-65—115
33-75 Thornell, 33-39-75—334
18-48 Thornton, 14-36-48—510
19-39 Thorpe, 9-19-39—764
08-37 Thula, 29-57-37—479

55-66 Thurman, 55-66-69—688
30-50 Thurston, 21-30-50—511
80-68 Tilda, 23-56-78—406
08-18 Tilden, 8-11-18—717
01-94 Tillery, 16-28-11—816
43-15 Tillie, 22-36-45—342
06-30 Tillman, 2-36-75—219
35-52 Tilly, 26-35-64—090
42-77 Timm, 31-52-77—753
85-67 Timothy, 11-59-67—156
11-22 Tinnon, 16-44-56—144
28-68 Tinsley, 28-50-68—441
76-91 Tipshaw, 6-39-61—109
10-70 Tito, 71-17-20—027
16-60 Tittle, 9-16-60—916
04-40 Titus, 4-15-40—321
39-58 Tobiah, 44-58-64—440
61-69 Tobias, 4-44-69—464
44-51 Tobie, 34-44-51—143
11-30 Tobin, 11-31-30—115
42-98 Tobitha, 7-27-54—665
92-29 Toburcio, 3-29-76—569
37-43 Toby, 9-37-43—675
34-56 Todd, 78-56-34—234
21-77 Toian, 51-72-77—727
90-60 Toinette, 10-23-60—602
35-72 Tolbert, 35-56-72—?76
03-33 Toledo, 40-33-54—543
46-66 Toler, 26-66-46—666
60-97 Toliver, 15-62-78—285
50-70 Tolston, 73-70-50—000
15-49 Tom, 3-15-49—868
39-89 Tomas, 43-39-13—139
15-41 Tommie, 55-41-15—115
50-75 Tompkins, 32-50-68—477
39-42 Toney, 42-39-37—974
14-39 Toni, 33-74-14—144
28-86 Tonia, 63-33-2&—836
08-18 Tony, 8-18-78—012
6-100 Topia, 6-16-66—679
26-20 Torbert, 24-26-20—262
35-65 Torcuato, 4-44-65—446
59-84 Torian, 29-59-61—198
08-96 Toribio, 12-75-8—857
29-49 Tormes, 41-64-49—944
12-79 Torre, 50-49-12—129
04-72 Torrence, 8-16-4—468
56-77 Torres, 43-56-77—756

34-40 Tottie, 25-34-40—043
12-19 Towers, 11-13-19—139
33-44 Townsend, 33-44-78—008
66-88 Toy, 33-66-55—543
36-56 Tracy, 19-36-56—019
14-27 Trauss, 56-65-27—726
37-68 Travis, 19-34-68—905
19-58 Trella, 26-76-19—197
34-95 Trewie, 34-45-67—009
44-73 Trice, 42-44-73—733
40-80 Trigg, 77-40-20—204
23-67 Trilby, 23-56-67—118
07-63 Trina, 11-32-63—323
16-34 Tris, 19-21-34—812
16-44 Trista, 21-53-16—155
36-62 Tristam, 5-36-62—264
02-71 Tristan, 17-7-37—737
23-53 Trix, 60-53-23—135
11-31 Trixy, 17-70-31—507
78-99 Trotter, 45-78-16—164
45-67 Troy, 15-45-67—862
57-92 Truda, 30-38-57—577
39-55 Trujillo, 54-69-39—998
23-45 Truman, 7-23-45—434
33-74 Trumbo, 15-74-34—740
26-84 Trumbull, 8-11-36—344
45-69 Tryphosa, 2-59-69—645
53-46 Tubau, 13-53-56—111
30-60 Tubbs, 30-31.-60—460
17-76 Tucker, 13-57-62—567
10-15 Turner, 10-15-24^—101
05-11 Turpin, 5-11-36—520
37-46 Twitty, 8-13-46—409
54-64 Tyce, 20-29-54—549
01-14 Tyler, 9-46-14—146
24-37 Tyrone, 14-37-24—738
61-46 Tyrus, 52-61-54—860
83-47 Tyson, 3-18-47—441

# U

31-56 Uda, 31-53-56-453
48-54 Uhler, 12-54-67—510
09-29 Ula, 1-9-29—452
29-36 Ulises, 29-36-6—764
47-93 Ulrica, 19-28-68—688
13-63 Ulrich, 13-63-78—633
10-21 Ulysses, 1-10-21—010
75-81 Una, 36-58-75—582

51-32 Undeen, 11-51-63—563
27-82 Underwood, 28-48-5—589
18-68 Undine, 47-68-18—186
07-77 Unice, 7-10-77—632
38-49 Upham, 23-53-67—887
32-44 Upp, 8-32-44—412
25-30 Upshaw, 14-39-58—879
52-61 Ura, 5-11-61—809
55-87 Urania, 8-13-56—400
02-19 Urban, 2-19-27—554
100-2 Urbank, 67-21-2—235
39-87 Uriah, 13-27-39—937
09-74 Uriel, 42-48-74 444
18-81 Urrabieta, 1-9-18—189
13-33 Urriola, 57-13-33—353
65-56 Urruti, 18-56-65—566
48-67 Ursa, 35-66-43—645
12-19 Ursaline, 8-19-56—018
26-52 Ursula, 49-52-26—264
05-57 Urvie, 5-10-57—571
56-94 Usher, 12-56-47—466
27-56 Utha, 3-43-56—546
06-12 Utopia, 6-12-33—761

# V

15-61 Vall, 18-61-15—511
55-80 Valcarcel, 5-38-55—823
02-23 Valdai, 52-70-23—705
74-93 Valdivia, 8-14-9—134
25-53 Vale, 25-28-53—355
48-86 Valeda, 61-46-23—246
14-21 Valencia, 28-37-21—278
39-49 Valentin, 36-48-59-400
08-16 Valentine, 8-16-42—342
60-68 Valeriano, 4-16-68—654
46-79 Valerie, 43-51-46—876
17-36 Valle, 7-17-36—771
48-58 Valley, 35-58-48—443
36-99 Valonia, 15-19-36—915
17-27 Valory, 27-36-47—367
47-54 Van, 36-54-47—452
45-67 Vance, 45-67-43—464
30-50 Vandane, 30-50-49—110
92-59 Vander, 38-66-59—496
32-45 Vanessa, 1-32-45—710
56-74 Vanesta, 3-19-74—154
13-42 Vanice, 14-62-42—548
39-59 Vanita, 19-39-59—993

07-50 Vanito, 7-35-50—054
27-47 Vann, 27-47-57—747
14-26 Vannice, 71-26-14—146
67-83 Vannie, 14-67-24—873
09-18 Vanolia, 9-18-48—630
18-41 Vanrie, 27-18-39—927
35-56 Vargas, 5-35-56—532
62-98 Varían, 26-62-54—463
37-91 Vasco, 42-37-63—373
33-67 Vasquez, 50-67-33—604
23-41 Vassar, 23-41-43—344
16-57 Vassie, 7-10-57—534
19-85 Vaughn, 6-13-55—418
01-12 Vaughns, 13-34-1—431
12-78 Veal, 12-47-78—748
30-57 Vearlena, 3-25-57—556
43-51 Veaster, 72-51-43—314
26-74 Vedla, 8-26-74—268
66-78 Vega, 33-66-78—776
29-36 Velasco, 41-54-29—547
73-97 Velma, 63-73-68—637
37-59 Velmor, 17-37-59—613
84-91 Venancio, 24-42-48—847
16-32 Venegas, 39-64-16—164
90-54 Venia, 24-54-60—046
06-38 Venias, 12-24-38—246
18-73 Vennie, 18-30-73—303
33-53 Venson, 5-31-53—551
25-65 Ventura, 55-65-25—556
11-44 Venus, 49-73-44—473
35-49 Venustiano, 53-8-35—823
11-56 Veora, 4-11-56—852
18-47 Vera, 5-18-47—819
36-56 Veradis, 17-39-36—576
09-22 Verda, 19-22-9—934
03-69 Verdugo, 9-29-69—299
62-75 Verdure, 60-62-75—562
81-94 Vergil, 44-78-18—187
41-54 Vergey, 24-54-41—543
25-70 Verlean, 13-25-70—476
46-61 Verlene, 14-46-61—416
41-73 Vermont, 41-58-73—355
34-43 Verlon, 34-43-53—883
26-87 Verna, 59-68-26-678
08-47 Verne, 77-47-8—743
3-100 Vemeda, 30-3-40—034
49-56 Vemell, 28-49-56—875
70-44 Vemellie, 1-44-70—704

34-40 Vemette, 45-34-40—344
09-19 Vemice, 9-19-37—876
30-60 Vemie, 8-18-60—790
25-46 Vemita, 34-38-25—339
15-76 Vernon, 7-15-76—965
28-64 Vernuce, 10-29-64—155
11-53 Verona, 11-25-62—361
95-65 Veronica, 20-67-65—576
23-61 Versa, 5-14-61—147
16-33 Vertie, 10-58-16—126
04-82 Vessie, 31-46-4—00
11-71 Vesta, 8-11-71—527
40-31 Vestie, 11-18-40—321
26-77 Veyola, 16-26-77—673
29-39 Vicente, 76-39-26—266
14-41 Vicey, 22-16-41—267
60-76 Vickers, 60-38-76—600
45-88 Vickie, 21-32-45—453
63-71 Vicky, 66-75-63—346
04-40 Victor, 4-10-40—672
40-56 Victoria, 8-17-56—221
23-40 Victoriano, 23-59-74—480
40-37 Victorino, 11-33-40—976
20-40 Victory, 47-57-20—027
96-54 Vida, 25-54-76—112
02-22 Villa, 2-11-22—163
17-54 Villegas, 2-22-54—378
52-76 Villena, 18-52-76—526
05-30 Vimes, 48-30-5—034
24-83 Vina, 65-24-38—248
39-72 Vincennes, 26-39-54—390
16-73 Vincent, 9-16-73—369
11-16 Vincente, 16-35-57—577
10-64 Vinson, 56-74-64—644
17-37 Viola, 9-17-37—721
77-89 Violet, 40-77-17—177
31-58 Violetta, 6-23-31—345
49-16 Violette, 10-16-49—106
58-23 Vira, 31-58-74—887
08-58 Virgie, 8-18-58—307
09-19 Virgil, 9-19-54—861
27-31 Virginia, 4-31-56—797
09-65 Viridis, 14-39-65—593
56-78 Virsie, 52-56-78—788
03-72 Vita, 23-33-72—247
39-63 Viuda, 9-39-63—139
14-31 Viudo, 14-20-31—024
06-66 Vivian, 6-5-66—863

16-48 Vivien, 16-34-53—164
39-26 Vivienne, 26-48-37—199
98-55 Vizconde, 27-38-49—01
86-60 Vladimir, 19-60-74—009
29-34 Volita, 7-34-29—619
12-37 Voshtie, 8-12-37—493

# W

64-46 Wabash, 46-48-49—490
25-75 Waddell, 13-25-75—400
11-38 Wade, 1-11-18—701
32-11 Wadsworth, 11-32-48—20
31-38 Wage, 31-38-52—312
11-65 Wagner, 11-31-65—069
52-78 Wakefield, 19-31-78—990
10-47 Waldemar, 8-30-32—320
30-61 Walden, 26-30-61—634
05-55 Waldo, 5-12-55—092
66-76 Walker, 37-40-46—655
16-45 Wallace, 8-16-45—165
62-87 Waller, 23-49-38—992
37-54 Wallington, 37-54-63—775
13-58 Walsh, 13-56-78—118
23-17 Walter. 17-23-30—799
79-94 Walters, 13-77-78—787
52-75 Walton, 8-31-52—009
04-46 Wanamaker, 15-32-1—193
29-71 Wanda, 35-71-39—331
13-35 Warbucks, 13-35-58—743
46-49 Ward, 46-57-76—780
17-67 Wardell, 62-31-58—761
11-56 Ware, 56-34-78—019
55-82 Warfield, 7-47-55—980
32-55 Waring, 32-55-67—599
61-88 Warmen, 6-8-72—212
99-59 Warner, 26-38-59-411
46-58 Warren, 46-58-72—212
14-18 Washington, 12-18-5—207
12-24 Waters, 12-24-20—200
34-74 Warford, 12-42-59—432
32-53 Watkins, 32-53-59—074
08-80 Watson, 14-35-74—477
28-45 Watton, 22-28-61—298
05-36 Watts, 16-23-37—137
89-95 Wayne, 6-19-56—717
18-66 Wealior, 18-34-66—843
32-40 Weatherall, 25-32-40—235
37-57 Weatherby, 37-46-48—887

51-15 Weatherly, 45-15—151
11-40 Weathers, 11-40-59—701
26-08 Weaver, 14-36-78—111
30-64 Webb, 77-30-29—880
85-62 Webster, 31-49-62—863
35-68 Weeks, 35-52-68—332
50-97 Weiser, 42-53-56—599
24-71 Welch, 20-24-71—027
07-14 Wellington, 7-14-66—702
14-40 Wells, 4-14-40—743
22-93 Wenceslao, 50-31-47—763
12-50 Wendell, 12-49-50—482
59-25 Wentworth, 13-19-36-495
10-66 Wesley, 6-10-66—900
02-14 Wess, 5-34-50—145
33-41 West, 11-32-8—887
84-38 Westbrook, 24-38-57—770
25-77 Weston, 35-65-77—440
45-10 Whalen, 29-45-75—110
59-73 Wheatley, 16-59-47—961
12-92 Whidbee, 12-20-33—332
18-70 Whitaker, 18-45-62—665
21-51 White, 32-53-56—566
43-58 Whitehall, 43-46-76—711
13-83 Whitehead, 54-42-35—888
33-77 Whitfield, 48-63-77—477
69-75 Whitmore, 58-75-69—703
20-36 Whitney, 3-20-36—362
26-96 Widget, 43-53-66—543
50-69 Wiggins, 13-50-69—118
42-55 Wilber, 26-42-55—246
02-21 Wilbem, 21-2-36—555
39-47 Wilbert, 39-41-47—147
60-69 Wilbur, 3-18-43—901
20-40 Wilburn, 20-40-65—420
34-82 Wilcox, 54-76-43—990
01-91 Wilder, 9-11-19—911
52-84 Wilderson, 14-52-8—152
27-43 Wildinson, 27-7-43—377
43-67 Wilett, 6-43-67—987
24-36 Wiletta, 24-36-57—577
42-67 Wiley, 45-67-42—612
40-55 Wilfred, 55-40-76—880
12-44 Wilhelmina, 4-12-44—234
07-68 Wilhemenia, 17-7-68—679
07-11 Will, 7-10-11—578
53-58 Willa, 32-53-58—444
55-90 Willamae, 67-45-32—792

15-42 Willamson, 42-5-15—556
35-81 Willard, 53-57-69—876
06-53 Willem, 26-53-66—362
87-27 Willester, 9-19-59—478
19-44 Willetta, 19-39-44—494
07-11 William, 7-10-11—578
07-11 Williams, 13-32-40—407
36-46 Williamson, 36-46-10—422
11-13 Williard, 13-52-57—776
07-11 Willie, 7-10-11—101
30-75 Willis, 16-29-75—195
14-44 Willister, 14-44-56—441
44-76 Willoby, 55-44-76—110
10-22 Willoughby, 5-10-22—102
97-39 Wills, 14-39-50—593
16-51 Willy, 16-51-62—217
43-63 Wilma, 35-43-63—633
59-76 Wilmette, 6-11-73—610
23-49 Wilova, 12-23-49—594
07-13 Wilson, 7-10-13—110
50-65 Winchell, 8-13-65—805
15-75 Winchester, 3-15-75—457
58-67 Winfred, 12-57-67—566
19-09 Wingate, 9-19-29—991
36-84 Winifred, 36-43-55—325
96-45 Winnie, 4-16-45—152
59-75 Winns, 4-31-59—544
07-77 Winona, 7-11-77—910
37-66 Winston, 14-44-56—538
11-53 Winters, 11-67-53—442
32-65 Wise, 32-53-65—701
30-89 Wolcott, 30-53-76—887
17-34 Wolfson, 3-17-34—433
10-12 Wood, 11-10-12—211
35-69 Woodard, 35-52-69—310
17-57 Wooden, 53-58-77—778
11-18 Woods, 11-10-18—301
95-48 Woodson, 32-55-78—441
04-74 Woody, 54-56-74—112
65-83 Woolfolk, 15-36-78—322
24-44 Wooten, 32-52-56—888
19-50 Worth, 19-20-50—809
18-36 Wren, 6-18-36—186
100-2 Wrenzo, 57-2-12—122
11-66 Wright, 7-11-66—666
66-73 Wrigley, 32-53-66—770
47-94 Wyatt, 40-47-49—944
28-08 Wrilla, 22-28-68—688

51-88 Wynn, 30-51-66—124

# X

36-82 Xavier, 36-54-56—980
18-56 Xenia, 7-18-56—435
03-56 Xeros, 3-53-65—90
64-83 Xerxes, 24-64-72—798

# Y

23-36 Yale, 23-36-56—543
35-46 Yancey, 1-35-36—158
12-72 Yancy, 4-51-58—421
08-27 Yanez, 8-11-27—505
25-58 Yantis, 32-58-75—69
33-38 Yardley, 11-33-38—311
14-57 Yards, 14-39-57—357
78-90 Yates, 53-56-78—732
20-54 Yolanda, 20-3-54—440
64-59 Yolette, 56-64-76—250
42-52 Young, 42-52-56—480
25-42 Youngman, 25-36-58—332
24-68 Ysabel, 24-42-52—442
01-11 Yunge, 1-11-74—411
06-31 Yvette, 42-36-47—332
10-40 Yvonne, 10-18-56—102

# Z

15-29 Zachariah, 36-46-42—312
22-35 Zachary, 35-22-55—253
11-22 Zachery, 4-22-50—891
33-36 Zackary, 11-33-36—455
52-78 Zacosta, 26-52-78—785
91-84 Zamora, 24-43-57—347

28-41 Zantha, 41-28-61—304
69-85 Zaszu, 26-69-70—709
05-28 Zebedee, 5-11-28—528
19-39 Zecilio, 19-39-48—004
14-20 Zeke, 10-14-20—140
42-50 Zelda, 34-42-50—423
28-53 Zelia, 14-11-18—181
25-35 Zelma, 25-35-53—-33
22-92 Zeman, 32-53-56—555
29-49 Zenith, 29-62-49—805
36-62 Zennetta, 13-62-41—818
45-11 Zenobia, 8-11-45—752
03-33 Zenola, 3-33-39—305
32-43 Zenon, 26-32-43—323
86-07 Zenteno, 77-16-7—716
19-27 Zephra, 19-27-38—739
62-70 Zephyr, 49-62-70—070
31-41 Zerlie, 41-31-51—888
44-93 Zetta, 53-44-26—246
80-99 Ziggy, 20-35-50—359
33-87 Zimmer, 3-33-39—355
32-33 Zimmerman, 1-32-56—441
55-69 Zipper, 52-56-69—432
08-13 Zoe, 19-13-8—138
63-71 Zoila, 26-63-71—776
15-19 Zola, 15-19-36—665
74-26 Zora, 35-74-78—310
81-55 Zorah, 13-55-46—100
44-55 Zorana, 5-44-55—110
26-41 Zula, 26-41-69—415
34-45 Zulen, 24-34-66—347
06-66 Zuletta, 6-15-66—325

WISDOM is the principal thing; therefore get wisdom:
and with all thy getting get UNDERSTANDING.
Prov. 4:7

# ARIES — The Ram

*From MARCH 21st to APRIL 19th*

| | |
|---|---|
| **Your Color** | Rose (Red) |
| **Lucky Day** | Thursday |
| **Birthstar** | Mars |
| **Guiding Prayer** | 30th Psalm |
| **Candle Colors** | Pink & Orange |
| **Birthroot** | Master of the Woods |
| **Birthstone** | Diamond |
| **Ruling Numbers** | 9-19-29-201 |

This is a most favorable sign to be born under, as the Aries people usually possess extraordinary character and are noted for their push, energy, and executive ability. They are therefore the natural leaders of humanity. As to earnestness and determination, they are unequaled. Yet with all their natural desire to rule and command, they are kind, gentle, noble, generous, agreeable, pleasing, magnetic, and progressive. Many secret powers are possessed by these Aries people, and the majority of them are deeply interested in occult and metaphysical studies. as latent within them are qualities which, if awakened, will give them wonderful force and power. Knowledge and deep thinking, with cultivation of the spiritual side of their nature, will cause them to achieve distinction and reach their highest attainment.

Patience is to be practiced by all Aries people. To know how to wait is the great secret of success. As a rule, these people are stubborn and like to do their work in their own way. The principal faults of Aries people are anger, impatience, and foolish generosity. They must be careful to guard against anger and jealousy, which will destroy their natural advantages. Within them is the light and power of the world. Their will is so strong and dominant, their sympathies so deep and kind, and they have such wonderful clairvoyant powers, that they can succeed in almost anything they undertake if they apply themselves and stick to it with perseverance and faith in God.

# TAURUS — The Bull

*From April 20th to May 19th*

| | |
|---|---|
| **Your Color** | Pearl (Blue) |
| **Lucky Day** | Tuesday |
| **Birthstar** | Venus |
| **Guiding Prayer** | 28th Psalm |
| **Candle Colors** | Blue & Gold |
| **Birthroot** | Low John the Conqueror |
| **Birthstone** | Emerald |
| **Ruling Numbers** | 61-48-35-391 |

Persons born under the sign of Taurus are remarkable people in many respects. They are generally fearless, kind, and gentle. They are continually thinking about doing good and would often like to help humanity more than they do. This desire to help others draws and attracts people and often makes, them respected leaders.

Many Taurus people are spiritualists, and many celebrated mediums and clergymen are found in this sign. They usually have rare clairvoyant gifts, which can often be used to help those in need of guidance.

Taurus people often anger easily and quickly as they are very sensitive to die people around them. They are very loyal to their friends, but they must be permitted to rule and have their own way; they will not stand much opposition, even from those near and dear to them. They always think their way is the best, and if there is any possible chance to carry out their plans, they will do so regardless of the results. However, having knowledge of the importance of self control, the more intellectual Taurus people do not give way to their weaknesses, and thus by cultivating their will, they become very powerful and successful.

A Taurus 'person who can thoroughly rule and control his lower or animal nature is a giant of power and can rule and govern great bodies of people. When the higher nature rules and dominates their lower or brutal instincts, Taurus people stand out as the personification of dignity, bravery, purity, and personal excellence.

# GEMINI — The Twins

*From May 20th to June 20th*

| | |
|---|---|
| **Your Color** | Emerald (Green) |
| **Lucky Day** | Saturday |
| **Birthstar** | Mercury |
| **Guiding Prayer** | 23rd Psalm |
| **Candle Colors** | Red & Blue |
| **Birthroot** | Japo Holy Root |
| **Birthstone** | Pearl & Moonstone |
| **Ruling Numbers** | 6-11-66-505 |

In most cases the Gemini People are dual in their natures. They are very happy, and they are very miserable, almost at the same time. They wish to work, and they wish to play. They want to travel, and they want to stay home. One minute they have a desire for wealth, and the next they are grateful and content to be as they are: One moment they love, the next moment they hate. There are no people more affectionate and generous; they are courteous, considerate, kind, and gentle to all. Their lower nature is very low, and their higher nature is very high. When the lower nature is subdued or dominated by the higher nature, these fine traits prevail and lead them to be the great people of the world.

Gemini people are generally eager to help others, and they often neglect their own affairs in assisting others. Sympathy for the suffering and thoughtfulness of the poor are strong inherent qualities.

One great fault of these people is that they usually spend or give away their money as fast as they earn it. Yet once they gain full control of all their desires and passions, there is almost nothing that they cannot do. They have the qualities to become excellent money earners and savers, and at the same time be able to help those in need. The change that takes place in the truly awakened Gemini is marvelous, and seems like a miracle. This is brought about through a sincere and honest desire to know the truth, combined with the highest aspirations to live the righteous life.

# CANCER — The Crab
*From June 21st to July 21st*

| | |
|---|---|
| **Your Color** | Orange |
| **Lucky Day** | Tuesday |
| **Birthstar** | The Moon |
| **Guiding Prayer** | 37th Psalm |
| **Candle Color** | Red & Green |
| **Birthroot** | Grains of Paradise |
| **Birthstone** | Ruby |
| **Ruling Numbers** | 41-38-60-701 |

It is often quite difficult to understand people born under the sign of Cancer, and very often these people go through life as puzzles to even their very closest friends. Some of die greatest people of the world have been Cancer born, on the other hand, some of the greatest failures were born under this sign.

Cancer people are naturally endowed with strong determination, intuition, and purpose, and if they will only persistently hold on and not give up and have an honest and sincere desire to conquer their faults, they may overcome all obstacles and attain great success.

People of this sign are generally restless and nervous, and their fondness for travel should be gratified whenever possible. By nature, Cancer people are very sympathetic and tender-hearted, and they are often overly generous. They are very weak when afraid, but they must understand that they have only their lower nature to fear. Their higher nature must be awakened; then will they realize their great possibilities. The planetary and solar conditions are very favorable to the awakened and dedicated and very unfavorable to those who wander in the dark.

During the day these people are in their most comfortable and happy moods, while at night they often become blue, depressed, and unhappy. At these times, when the world does not look very bright, and they are perplexed, nervous, and restless, they should seek some quiet spot and silently meditate on the higher things in life and seek contentment and peace within themselves.

# LEO — The Lion

*From July 22nd to August 21st*

| | |
|---|---|
| **Your Color** | Yellow |
| **Lucky Day** | Monday |
| **Birthstar** | The Sun |
| **Guiding Prayer** | 39th Psalm |
| **Candle Colors** | Pink & Orange |
| **Birthroot** | Mojoe Bean |
| **Birthstone** | Sardonyx or Onyx |
| **Ruling Numbers** | 12-15-32-108 |

Leo people are kind-hearted, generous, sympathetic, and magnetic. Their great love and tenderness makes them loved by all and gives them a charm and personality that is felt wherever they go. They are highly emotional and generally very intuitive. They are quick to see a point, and they are equally quick to make one.

Leo people, owing to their natural goodness, tend to create a calm, peaceful, and happy atmosphere around them, when their dominant higher nature prevails. Many of them seem to be endowed with a spiritual light that attracts those in need, for Leo's are wonderful people to inspire others to do good. When the whole nature of a Leo person has yielded and becomes subject unto its higher self, it becomes a giant of will-power and force.

Courage is the noble trait of Leo people, and that power over the mind that enables them to bear up under all danger and difficulties commands the highest admiration and respect. A great deal of misery and suffering is brought on some Leo people by their strong affection and passion for the opposite sex. When the lower nature prevails in the undeveloped person, the bad faults dominate the good ones. They may be impatient, impetuous, hot headed, easy to anger, and irritable, which often alienates those that they wish to attract. When vexed with troubles, these people would do well to go into silence, calm themselves, and ask for light and direction from a Higher Power that can bring them new strength, new life, and new force.

# VIRGO — The Virgin

*From August 22nd to September 22nd*

| | | |
|---|---|---|
| **Your Color** | Amber | |
| **Lucky Day** | Wednesday | |
| **Birthstar** | Mercury | |
| **Guiding Prayer** | 32nd Psalm |  |
| **Candle Colors** | Rose & Gold | |
| **Birthroot** | Southern John Conqueror | |
| **Birthstone** | Sapphire | |
| **Ruling Numbers** | 3-6-20-632 | |

The sign of Virgo represents the hidden fire of the earth, and persons born under it are remarkable for their orderly and methodical habits, which reveals them to have the above average qualities and abilities of a thinking and observing person. These people generally enjoy the pleasures of religious guidance as they are able to see their problems in a clear light. Their unbounded faith and enthusiasm are their vital forces that help them to meet adversity and difficulties should they come their way. The awakened Virgo people are never discouraged for they can surmount and overcome any obstacles. They must examine their faults and errors, for in this way there is much benefit to be found in their experience that will lead them to the success and happiness they seek.

The very highest types of Virgo people, and the most forceful for good, are those in which the intellectual side is cultivated as well as the spiritual. This type of person is wonderfully charming, enchanting, and powerful. Such a person can take advantage of the tremendous possibilities that lie before all those born under this sign.

Virgo people make many sacrifices for their families and friends often to their own hardship. In spite of their generous natures, they often find that material rewards are small, and they must return to the gratifying rewards to be found in their faith that after die storm has passed, die Almighty will hear and grant their prayers, for they are die pure of heart and the righteous.

# LIBRA — The Scales
*From September 23rd to October 21st*

| | |
|---|---|
| **Your Color** | Crimson (Red) |
| **Lucky Day** | Thursday |
| **Birthstar** | Venus |
| **Guiding Prayer** | 23rd Psalm |
| **Candle Colors** | Pink & Gold |
| **Birthroot** | King Solomon |
| **Birthstone** | Opal & Tourmaline |
| **Ruling Numbers** | 10-30-70-223 |

People born under this sign are naturally ambitious, energetic, and inspired. Libra people are bold and daring in their enterprises and can bear up under losses and ill luck better than those born under other signs because their higher nature tends to be dominant.

Libra people are ever anxious for new interests and new enterprises. Their dynamic spiritual faith gives them the strength and guidance to overcome adversity and difficult times. There are no people who have more hope and enthusiasm.

The diversity of their interests brings them in contact with many people who need their help, and the natural generosity, spiritually and financially of Libra people generally prevails. When spiritualized or awakened to the higher duties of man, the scales hang evenly balanced, and the good that these people can do is phenomenal.

People of this sign are very finely constituted, and the result is that they are often over-sensitive and afraid of disaster to those near them. For these over-sensitive souls, it is best for them to learn to adapt themselves to conditions and circumstances over which they have no control.

The Libra birthstar, Venus, lends to intuition, good judgment, and love of music and the arts as well as humans and animals. Around Libra people are the most wonderful magnetic forces, which endows them with great psychic power, which with their exceedingly keen perception makes no goal too high to reach. Take courage in your faith.

# SCORPIO — The Scorpion

*From October 22nd to November 21st*

| | |
|---|---|
| **Your Color** | Scarlet (Red) |
| **Lucky Day** | Saturday |
| **Birthstar** | Mars |
| **Guiding Prayer** | 37th Psalm |
| **Candle Colors** | Yellow & Blue |
| **Birthroot** | European John Conqueror |
| **Birthstone** | Topaz |
| **Ruling Numbers** | 7-11-77-102 |

Scorpio people are very wonderful in many respects, since they are possessed with marvelous vibratory forces, which give them great vitality. This power is so pronounced in most persons of this sign that they are generally very strong in soothing and consoling powers that can benefit all those closely connected with them who are in need of comfort and guidance.

By nature, these people possess indomitable will, and they have the greatest self-control. They are noted for their cool courage in the face of hardship and emergencies.

The educated and cultured Scorpio people use great tact and care in dealing with people and situations, and they usually have much force and influence over all with whom they come in contact. There are none more helpful than Scorpio people when they are fully developed.

Most of these people have a quiet, dignified, superior manner, which generally inspires confidence and admiration. These qualities must be enhanced and favored for they are great factors in helping them to success and happiness.

When awakened and spiritualized, they take on added strength, being helpful, powerful, kind, gentle, and considerate, and doing everything in their power to help humanity. But if they are entirely engrossed in money-making, their lower nature prevails, and they can be very selfish and mean. When these faults are corrected, their higher nature will prevail, and there is little that can stand in the way of happiness and prosperity.

# SAGITTARIUS — The Archer

*From November 22nd to December 20th*

| | |
|---|---|
| **Your Color** | Red |
| **Lucky Day** | Friday |
| **Birthstar** | Jupiter |
| **Guiding Prayer** | 29th Psalm |
| **Candle Colors** | Red & Orange |
| **Birthroot** | Adam & Eve |
| **Birthstone** | Turquoise |
| **Ruling Numbers** | 16-48-32-606 |

People born under this sign are remarkable in many ways. In the first place, they are generally observant and far-sighted. They can generally foresee future occurrences and can prepare to handle any eventuality in an orderly, efficient manner. When they rely on their own judgment, they are more likely to be successful than when they take the advice of those often less gifted in wisdom than themselves.

One of the outstanding qualities of Sagittarius people is their knowledge of the advantages of attending strictly to their own business. They are very active and energetic people, which is an important factor in maintaining their mental and physical health.

People born in this sign have a tendency to become very angry and upset over relatively trivial and unimportant matters. The highly developed people of this sign learn to suppress their anger, yet they tend to remember an injury a long time. They must learn to cultivate calmness and repose, and thus place themselves in a quiet, calm, and thoughtful state so that the wonderful spiritual and planetary forces from within may surge forward, giving them tremendous strength, vigor, wisdom, and knowledge.

This is also a musical and an occult sign, and those who are spiritualized make wonderful leaders. It is very wise indeed for Sagittarius people to give attention to religious and spiritual matters, as when their higher self is awakened, they reveal a powerful and lovable quality which assures that much joy, peace, and happiness may be theirs.

# CAPRICORN — The Goat

*From December 21st to January 20th*

| | |
|---:|:---|
| **Your Color** | Red |
| **Lucky Day** | Monday |
| **Birthstar** | Saturn |
| **Guiding Prayer** | 29th Psalm |
| **Candle Colors** | Red & Gold |
| **Birthroot** | Paradise Seed |
| **Birthstone** | Garnet |
| **Ruling Numbers** | 1-30-72-178 |

This is the dark or mysterious sign of the earth. Within Capricorn is solitude, meditation, and the occult side of history. Capricorn people are naturally inclined to study and deep thinking, producing some of the world's greatest scholars and teachers. People of this sign usually give much attention to the cultivation of the mind and the admiration of intellect. They realize that through the development of their mental facilities and the consummation of knowledge in all fields lies the path to success and happiness.

Capricorn people are very hard workers; the handicap of their higher nature being that they try to do too many things at once, which tires and wears them down physically and mentally. They must learn that true and lasting success comes from concentrating all their forces and energies to the completion of the task at hand. These people resent interference of others who tell them how to run their affairs, and for this reason they realize that they should not meddle in the affairs of others. At times Capricorn people are very brilliant and alive with confidence and exuberance; at times they are morbidly depressed and melancholy. But they are philosophically and religiously inspired, and they soon rally from the blues to again encounter and conquer the tasks at hand. The most successful are those who realize the relative value of matter and soul, material things and spirit, and enhance their lives by giving each a proper proportion of their attention.

# AQUARIUS — The Water Bearer

*From January 21st to February 19th*

| | |
|---:|:---|
| **Your Color** | Pink |
| **Lucky Day** | Friday |
| **Birthstar** | Uranus |
| **Guiding Prayer** | 59th Psalm |
| **Candle Colors** | Yellow & Blue |
| **Birthroot** | High John The Conqueror |
| **Birthstone** | Amethyst |
| **Ruling Numbers** | 10-18-40-119 |

The very strongest and the very weakest people in the world are generally born under this sign. The strength and power of Aquarius people lies within their own hands, as they can make of themselves what they choose. They can either achieve the best or highest things or be complete failures. By nature, these people are endowed with great possibilities. They possess unusual powers and abilities, but they are often too lazy to use them. If they would only wake up, use the talents of their higher nature, and live up to their honest, kind, wise, and excellent judgment abilities, they could pave the way to success and happiness.

The awakened or regenerated Aquarius people are exceedingly active, industrious, and dominating over the forces that determine their lot in life. They are not easily deceived, and they are generally good readers of character. They will earnestly seek advice from others, and then generally go about their business as they see fit.

By nature, they are very pleasing and agreeable people, attempting to be proper and dignified on all occasions. As a rule the higher nature of Aquarius people prevails, and they are calm and peaceful with excellent control of their angry passions. To a remarkable degree, they possess the power of inspiration and divination, called the power of the Holy Ghost. When their souls are aroused to spiritual and divine truth, then improvement along every line is marvelous, and the highest general development generally follows.

# PISCES — The Fishes

*From February 20th to March 20th*

| | | |
|---|---|---|
| **Your Color** | Emerald (Green) | |
| **Lucky Day** | Wednesday |  |
| **Birthstar** | Neptune | |
| **Guiding Prayer** | 31st Psalm | |
| **Candle Colors** | Blue & Green | |
| **Birthroot** | Paradise Seed | |
| **Birthstone** | Bloodstone | |
| **Ruling Numbers** | 31-20-60-132 | |

The sign of Pisces denotes a deep, hidden love of nature, and all who are born under it are naturally noble, generous, and desirous of helping all in need. These people are natural lovers, and their love is generally high and pure, and their realm is the kingdom of the soul.

Their great desire to help people, which is prompted by intense love, often causes them to give too much of their time, physical effort, and finances, and thus deplete or weaken their own resources. The boundless love of Pisces people often leads them to be deceived through too much faith in human nature, especially by their "friends." They are exceedingly loyal, and they can rarely see the faults of those closest and dearest to them. They should be on their guard and use good judgment and common sense in sharing the blessings of their higher nature with others. When this higher or spiritual nature of Pisces people is developed, they are naturally honest, and they tend to keep their minds pure and clean, making them lovable people who are bound to attract the presence of those who appreciate these virtues.

Often Pisces people get tired and worn out with wearing the yoke of everyone else's burdens along with their own. Generally, they eventually rebel and suddenly become stubborn and disgusted. The one dominant relief from this unfavorable condition is silence and concentration, placing trust and faith in the Eternal God, that fear, doubt, weakness, and illness may vanish, and peace and happiness may reign.

Made in the USA
Columbia, SC
29 September 2022

68005513R00052